CREATIVE ACTIVITIES FOR CHILDREN IN THE EARLY PRIMARY GRADES

MARY MAYESKY

*North Carolina Department
of Human Resources
Office of Day Care Services*

 Delmar Publishers Inc.

To Mom and Dad, who gave me life
as well as the greater part of their own lives
unselfishly and lovingly,
I dedicate this book in deep appreciation.
M.M.

Delmar Staff:
   Administrative Editor: Karen Lavroff
   Production Editor: Carol Micheli

For information, address Delmar Publishers Inc.
2 Computer Drive West, Box 15015
Albany, New York 12212–5015

Printed in the United States of America
Published simultaneously in Canada by
Nelson Canada, a division of
International Thomson Limited

10   9   8   7   6   5   4   3   2

Library of Congress Cataloging in Publication Data

Mayesky, Mary.
    Creative activities for children in the early primary
grades.

    Bibliography: p.
    Includes index.
    1. Education, Primary. 2. Creative activities and
seat work. I. Title.
LB1140.2.M4   1986   372.5   85–12948
ISBN 0–8273–2573–8

Contents

Preface

CREATIVE ACTIVITIES FOR CHILDREN IN THE EARLY PRIMARY GRADES is the result of the author's deep involvement and commitment to school-age day care and the primary years in early childhood education. Over the years in the field of early childhood education, it seems that there has been less of an emphasis on young children at the primary end of the early childhood spectrum—those children in grades 1–3—than there has been on infants, toddlers, and preschoolers.

Yet, the field of early childhood education traditionally encompasses birth to age 8. And it is a fact that children ages 5–8 are still *young* children whose developmental needs do not disappear when they enter an elementary school. However, when children enter first grade far too often their developmental needs as young children take second place to a subject matter emphasis and the school curriculum in general.

This text is designed to meet the needs of these young children by providing a developmental approach to the subject areas usually taught in the primary grades. The emphasis is on understanding *how* young children learn, *what* to teach them, and *how to teach* the traditional subjects such as language arts and mathematics in a way that is developmentally appropriate for them.

As in its companion volume, CREATIVE ACTIVITIES FOR YOUNG CHILDREN, the emphasis in CREATIVE ACTIVITIES FOR CHILDREN IN THE EARLY PRIMARY GRADES is on using creative activities to teach concepts that mesh subject areas as well as help young children reach their fullest creative potential in the process. A multitude of activities for the subject areas of math, language arts, social studies, health, and nutrition are provided in this text to give those who work with primary children lots of ideas on how to make learning effective and fun.

The author's involvement in school-age day-care programs has made it very clear that there is a great need for appropriate activities and materials for this rapidly growing school-age day-care population. Many current early childhood activity books designed for preschool day care do not meet the needs of the school-age child. The activities in each unit of CREATIVE ACTIVITIES FOR CHILDREN IN THE EARLY PRIMARY GRADES are designed especially for school-age children in grades 1–3. It is also written to assist adults who work with school-age day-care programs provide creative, fun, learning experiences by emphasizing the following points:

- The approach to subject areas is a practical one. A wide variety of activities is included in each section. All activities have been successfully classroom-tested with school age children, grades 1–3.
- Information on *why* activities should be carried out as well as on *how* to carry them out is presented. Theory is provided for each of the subject areas, explaining the learning process for each.
- Learning activities and skill builders are included in each unit to help readers experience their own creativity.
- References for additional reading are given at the end of each unit so students can explore each subject in more depth as desired.
- Each unit begins with carefully worded, easy-to-understand objectives and ends with review questions.

Units in this text include the following:

- Language arts—including sections on children's books and non-sexist materials for children
- Langauge arts activity unit—meshing language arts with other subjects
- Mathematics—basic processes in learning mathematics
- Special topics in math—including math and block building, math and children's books, movement activities to teach math
- Social studies, part I—developing an understanding of self
- Social studies, part II—developing an understanding of others
- Health and nutrition
- Field trips—including sample lesson plans, forms, letters, tips

All units include activities, art ideas, games, songs, poetry, food experiences, finger plays, and suggested lesson plans related to each subject area as well as to individual concepts within each subject area. Photographs of children's work provide further creative ideas to use with primary grade children. A variety of diagrams giving step-by-step direction for making selected projects further aids in using the text.

Introduction

There go the grownups
To the office,
To the store,
Subway rush,
Traffic crush;
Hurry, scurry,
Worry, flurry.

No wonder
Grownups
Don't grow up
Any more.

It takes a lot
Of slow
To grow.
                    —Eve Merriam*

Young children, like the adults in this poem, are often rushed through their first years in school to learn reading, writing, and math. Yet the development of a young child is a unique, individual process. Each child has his or her own special rate of growth—intellectually, socially, emotionally, and physically. This process must not be pushed just to meet adult standards.

As the poem says, it takes time, or "a lot of slow," for a young child to develop understanding and gradual mastery of the traditional school subjects like math, reading, and writing. In the early childhood preschool years a child develops basic ideas such as numbers, letters, size, and order, which will be the basis for further learning in the primary grades. For example, understanding the concepts of "larger" and "smaller" is necessary to a young child's learning math (which is larger—5 or 8?) as well as learning to write capital and small (uppercase and lowercase) letters. Teaching math, writing, or any other subject to young children requires a knowledge of their developmental needs. Knowing just where each child is in his or her understanding and building on this level of understanding with appropriate learning activities is essential in the early elementary grades.

This text is designed for use with *young* children in the early elementary grades. "Young" is emphasized here because it is too often the case that a child in the first, second, or even third grade is not really considered young. Yet the early childhood years encompass the period from birth through age eight. And in these years, while children may be grouped together in a grade level, they are in fact at many different levels intellectually, socially, and emotionally. The early childhood emphasis on meeting developmental needs of individual children must, therefore, be present in the early elementary years just as in the preschool years. These are all *young* children, a fact which must temper all our teaching in the early elementary grades.

An equally important reason for developing this text was to meet the needs of the rapidly growing school-age day-care population. With the ever-increasing number of working and single parents, many school-age children are spending their time before and after school in day-care settings. Their needs are very different from those of preschool children, and this book is designed to help their caregivers and teachers plan exciting and challenging activities to enrich their experience.

In the units that follow, the basic developmental needs of young children are discussed for each subject area. The units are not intended to replace instruction in subjects such as reading, mathematics, or science but to provide a developmental approach to the teaching of these subjects in the early childhood years extending to grade 3.

It Doesn't Always Have to Rhyme. New York: Atheneum, 1962.

Unit 1 Language Arts

OBJECTIVES

After studying this unit, you will be able to

- list the two components of expressive language and give at least two examples of appropriate activities for each skill.
- list the components of receptive language and give at least two examples of appropriate activities for each skill.
- describe the development of spelling skills and give an example of each stage of invented spelling.
- list the basic characteristics of a good language arts program.

Language arts is the part of the curriculum that assists the child in the development of language skill. Language arts is one of the most important aspects of the early elementary years, as it is related to all aspects of the curriculum. This is so since they all involve words. In listening, ideas are received through words; in speaking and writing, ideas are expressed through words; and in reading, ideas are communicated through words. Although language arts is a very complex topic and involves many very specific skills, such as phonics, syllabication, and structural analysis, this unit will cover only three broad areas of language arts. These areas are: (1) expressive language, including speaking and writing; (2) receptive speech, involving listening and reading; and (3) writing, including the forming of letters and simple composing. For students desiring more in-depth information on these three areas, several sources for further reading are listed at the end of this unit.

EXPRESSIVE LANGUAGE: SPEECH

Speaking, or oral communication, is influenced by, and influences, every other aspect of development. A child must be able to speak in order to interact socially with others. A child who can express feelings verbally will generally make better social adjustments. A child's mental development is closely tied to development in oral communication.

The pattern of children's speech is established before they enroll in elementary school. The language that children bring to school mirrors the language of their homes and the educational and cultural background of their parents.

By age five, most children's speech resembles adult language in two important ways: (1) sentences are longer and more complex than before and (2) more than one idea is expressed in a single sentence. By the age of six, a child has learned most of the adult patterns of speech and has accomplished an impressive feat in acquiring such a tremendously complex skill.

Children's vocabularies also indicate the extent of their experiences, real and vicarious; therefore, the teacher must accept and use the language children bring with them, and provide opportunities and experiences to stimulate talking rather than repress it.

In the early elementary grades it is often possible to detect speech problems and give children early assistance in overcoming these problems. If signs of speech problems seem to be present, children should be referred to a speech therapist for help. The following guidelines are suggested:

- If a child shows signs of hearing problems, make arrangements for a hearing test.
- Work with ordinary speech problems common to young children. Refer only severe speech problems to a specialist. Children with only a lisp or defective *r, l, k,* or *g* can usually overcome these speech problems without special assistance.
- Accept as normal children with foreign accents and different dialects.

- Consult a speech therapist about all stuttering cases.

Teaching speech skills does not require a formal, teacher-directed setting where the child sits and listens passively and then responds to the teacher's questions. Children learn to speak best when they are actively engaged in doing something of real interest to them and relating their physical activity to appropriate speech. They are motivated to practice language in natural settings. Language competencies are enhanced by activities that encourage cooperation and interaction, such as cooking, dramatic play, and similar group projects.

Teachers can help stretch a child's verbal abilities by using a wide variety of expressions. Instead of saying, "Claire, think of another way to do that," the teacher might say, "Claire, have you considered other possibilities?" Claire may not be able to define all the teacher's words but will be challenged in a nonthreatening way to think about the meanings of those words in their context.

Children learn to speak by speaking. Opportunities to practice through conversations with adults are especially important. Following are some basic principles for facilitating children's speech:

- Children talk more if there is something of importance (to them) to talk about.
- Provide activities that lend themselves to verbal interaction, and relate verbal exchange to the real world when possible.
- Connect words or phrases to actions or demonstrations rather than to other words or phrases.
- Use language that is slightly more precise and complex than that which the child is now using.
- Informative comments evoke responses from children more often than commands or directives.
- For children who do not talk easily, structured situations may make them more comfortable.

Teaching Strategies to Encourage Speech. Listen to teacher–child talk for a while and certain patterns will become clear. With some adults, the tendency is to lean toward the interview technique: "What is your name?" "How old are you?" "Where do you live?" and so forth. These questions, by their very structure, usually prompt simple one- or two-word replies. The teacher who

consciously picks up on topics and activities that are of interest to the children will get many more elaborate verbal responses. For example, "Tell me about your favorite friend," or "What's it like to be at a party?" When the topic is of importance to the child, he is much more likely to become engaged in conversation.

Teachers also need to be sensitive to any tendencies to carry on a monologue. For example, giving directions ("Put the books away"), making comments ("I like what you're doing"), and giving warnings ("Be careful not to spill") constitute much of a teacher's verbalization during a school day. Such utterances do not encourage extended conversation. Teachers have to monitor themselves and plan an environment where good verbal interaction *can* take place.

Good verbal interaction takes place when teachers ask open-ended questions ("What do you suppose Mary wanted to do?") and make comments that encourage thinking responses ("I wonder why that happened . . ."). These strategies are likely to encourage children to respond with more conversation, rather than one- or two-word replies.

The teacher who is most likely to succeed in motivating children to speak is the one who listens very carefully to the child and watches for clues to the child's interests and concerns. Attending totally to children means not finishing their sentences for them or assuming that you already know what they want to say. Ask children to elaborate and explain what they mean when they make comments. For example, a child might complain that another "won't share." Ask the child to explain in greater detail. When children expand on their ideas in this way, they gain practice in verbalizing and they also clarify their thought processes for themselves and others.

Activities to Encourage Speech. The following activities to encourage speaking can be used in the language arts period of the early childhood program. Additional suggestions are given at the end of this unit.

- Divide children into small groups and give a picture to each group for discussion. Snapshots the children bring from home should encourage children to talk as their pictures are shown to the group.
- View a film or filmstrip, but do not include the sound. Instead, have the children make up the story.

- Have a brainstorming session. In such a session, thought-provoking questions are asked; answers are brainstormed by a small group of children and then shared with the larger group. The questions might be realistic or nonsense questions. Examples include:

  1. What new machine would you like to invent?
  2. What would you do if you could only walk backwards?
  3. What would be more beautiful if it were red?
  4. What would you do if you woke up one morning to a backyard full of penguins?
  5. If you only had one wish, what would it be?
  6. What would you buy if you could buy anything in the whole world?
  7. What would you like to do if you didn't go to school?
  8. What changes would you like to make in yourself?
  9. What if everyone had a long neck like a giraffe?

- After field trips, food activities, science activities, or visitors, have the children verbally summarize the experiences. Write this summary in the form of a story on a chart or chalkboard to be read back to the children. Pictures can be added to relate to each line.
- After a story that has had a definite sequence of events, have the children recall the events in the order they occurred.
- Have one child start to tell a story and the next child add on to it.
- Brainstorm items within a category. For example, after you say the word "animal," the children brainstorm all the animals they can remember. Be sure to encourage each child to offer one.
- Give the children various "Tell me . . ." statements and encourage brainstorming. Examples: "Tell me what colors the sky can be." "Tell me how many things you can wear on your head." "Tell me things that are big."
- Have each child pick an object out of a paper bag and describe the object.
- Have each child pick out a favorite storybook character for the class to guess, using a "20 Questions" format. That is, the child gives clues to the character and classmates ask questions.

EXPRESSIVE LANGUAGE: WRITING

The second major skill of expressive language is writing. The term "writing" includes both the forming of letters and the skill of composing, called written expression. For purposes of our discussion, we will refer to the forming of letters as writing. The term "composing" will be used in reference to written expression.

Writing includes a wide range of skills from the simple holding of a pencil through the forming of letters and words all the way to putting one's ideas into written form. The ability to write also reflects the child's emotional, physical, and intellectual development.

In our discussion we will focus on the motor coordination involved in writing. You may wish to consult the references at the end of this unit for further reading on other aspects of the development of writing skills.

Hand–eye coordination and small motor development are involved in the ability to write. The ability to write also involves these other visual motor skills:

- Eye movement from left to right.
- Recognizing and naming shapes.
- Relating right and left.
- Learning to follow a pattern and change direction.

Typically, young children in kindergarten (and possibly even earlier) are eager to learn how to write their own names and other words of special interest to them, such as names of TV cartoon characters, movie stars, and favorite sports teams.

Be sure that these and any other writing activities do not cause a child undue frustration or anxiety if they are less than successful. Encouraging many other forms of small motor activities is essential in the language arts writing program. For example, setting up a writing center as outlined in Figure 1–1 creates a place where children are encouraged to practice small motor skills required in writing. Playing with clay, tearing and cutting paper, crayoning and painting, using pegs and small blocks—these all provide practice with small motor skills in preparation for writing tasks. These activities are also pleasant, relaxing activities for the beginning writer.

Most important of all, the emphasis should be on fitting writing activities to the child's level of skill. Forced practice that is beyond the child's level of skill has no place in the writing program.

Center Functions and Goals

This center affords the child experiences in:

Kindergarten

- Developing legible letter forms.
- Expressing thoughts through individually and group-dictated writing.

Early Elementary

- Writing simply, spontaneously, and creatively.
- Composing poetry.
- Evaluating and refining spelling or written work.

Materials

Chalkboard, individual slates
Alphabet letter stamps and stamp pads
Paper
Pencils, crayons, markers, chalk, paintbrushes, scissors
Pictures
Blank books of assorted sizes and shapes (teacher-made)
Teacher-made task cards and materials
Word boxes
Pictionaries
Dictionaries
Flannel board and letters
Magnetic board and letters
Paste, glue, brads

FIGURE 1–1 Sample writing center

My Sister

Sometimes she cries.
Her name is Bonnie.
She's sick,
My mama makes her
    take the medicine.
She don't like it.
She don't like my mama
    to whip her.

> Mike
> Age 5
> Reading School

The Easter Bunny

Here comes the Easter bunny
Hop, hop, hop down the trailway.
People say that Easter's here,
But that ain't true.
I think you should wait to get
    your Easter basket until
    Easter gets here.

> Sherri
> Age 5
> Reading School

FIGURE 1–2 Individually dictated stories

Composing. Written expression involves the skills of observing, listening, and speaking. The skill of thinking precedes composing and also determines the quality of the child's written expression.

The teacher must create an atmosphere that stimulates children to compose, using common class experiences as well as personal experiences outside the school, and must develop the children's background for composing through books and other experiences.

While composing *form* is important, it should never be achieved at the cost of the original expression of the writer. There should always be an underlying respect for the child's ideas, ways of thinking, and self-expression. When children sense that their work is valued, they are more likely to write and to find pleasure in the activity.

Usual Sequence of Development in Composition. There is a general sequence for the development of composition in the early grades, as follows:

1. Provide a rich background of language experience with such activities as: cooking, tasting, smelling, enjoying a classroom mystery, making comparisons.
2. Provide initial composing experiences through individually and group-dictated exercises. For example: telling about a field trip, writing a letter to a friend, writing about the circus, labeling and describing pictures, building word charts (see Figures 1–2 and 1–3).
3. Provide opportunities for simple, spontaneous, independent writing such as: writing rainy day thoughts on an appropriate day; guiding sensory imagery with

FIGURE 1–3 Writing invitations to class parties is a good composing and handwriting activity.

FIGURE 1–4 Children choose books that are of interest to them as a natural part of the early childhood program.

concrete objects; putting thoughts in sequence; writing letters and greeting cards.

4. Provide opportunities for fanciful writing such as: following up fairy tales, fables, myths, and tall tales with their own versions; making up advertisements, jokes, and riddles; writing secrets.
5. Provide opportunities for simple poetry writing. Have children write in free style, remembering it is the idea that is important. Compose a class poetry book on selected topics of interest to the class.

Children at any stage of this sequence are not going to compose much unless they have something worthwhile to write about. You can add to the multitude of ideas children bring with them to school in a variety of ways: by reading to children; giving them time to observe, appreciate, and talk about things; giving them books in profusion and the opportunity to read them; giving attention to expressive words and apt phrases; and presenting concrete materials, objects, pictures, and sounds. Most of all children can be urged to capitalize on their own real experiences, in and out of school.

Motivation for Composing. Composing needs the climate and conditions for dealing with happenings as they occur,

plus a considerable store of ideas for helping them along. In a classroom climate free of criticism and full of respect for the child, the creative writing center for composing becomes a busy place where the students find and use:

- Different sizes, shapes, and colors of paper.
- Different kinds of pencils, crayons, colored chalk and pencils, magic markers.
- Old slate boards cut into 15″ X 18″ pieces to be used as lapboards.
- Acetate sheets for practice tracing over correct letter formation.
- Multiple sources of words: pictionaries, dictionaries, word lists, word boxes, and word charts pertaining to size, color, texture, shape, and so on.

You must plan many ways to bring new words into the child's oral vocabulary and then help make them a part of the child's written vocabulary. There are many ways you can create a mood to put new, colorful words into oral and written vocabulary:

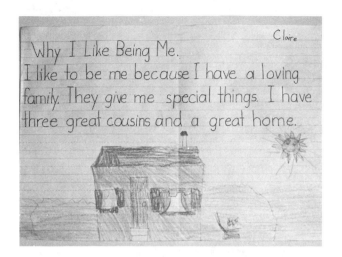

FIGURE 1–5   Language arts stories provide children with a chance to share their world with others.

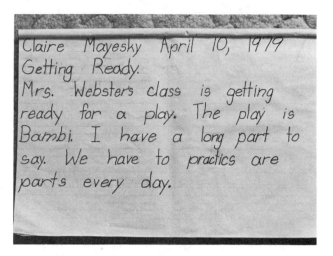

FIGURE 1–6   Happenings in the classroom make natural topics for composing.

- Play some evocative music. While it is playing have children write what first comes to mind (or dictate it, if necessary).
- Ask children to make a list of smells they like.
- Children can write answers to questions such as these:
  "What is happiness?"
  "What color is excitement and why?"
  "What is beauty?"
- Read poetry or stories.
- Dramatize a scene.
- Use voice changes in oral reading to emphasize mood, and describe or have children describe those changes.
- Set up a classroom post office.
- Coordinate composing with other areas of the curriculum.

The following quotation aptly summarizes the skill of composing and its importance to young children:

> Writing starts from ideas—and children are full of ideas. Creative ideas are those we believe in so strongly that they pound on the inner door to be released. It does not matter whether a teacher assigned the writing or we assigned it to ourselves: if we feel it, we can be taught to write it. Writing without feeling is anemic and bloodless, and the writer has no pride in it. Creative writing, then, is writing that pushes itself out of a bed of ideas. . . .
> (Applegate, 1963)

Spelling as Part of Composing.   Just as children develop in their ability to speak, read, and write, their proficiency at spelling has its own particular stages.   At the very beginning of learning to spell, children "invent" spellings. They start to write by representing words with single letters.   Gradually they move on to more phonetic spelling, and finally to conventional spelling.   (See Figures 1–7 and 1–8.)   The child's attempts to invent spelling need to be encouraged, as they are the basis of learning to spell.

Spelling is a skill that varies greatly in any group of children, and an individualized spelling program is highly desirable.   A plan that does not focus on learning to spell lists of words, but allows pupils to diagnose spelling errors by themselves in original writing is far more likely to produce the desired results.

The degree of success children experience in learning to spell is affected by:

- The attitude of the teacher and the child.
- The freedom children have to express their ideas and thoughts in writing.
- The degree to which spelling is taught in the total curriculum.
- The child's basic word recognition skills.
- The child's auditory and visual discrimination.
- Legibility of the child's handwriting.

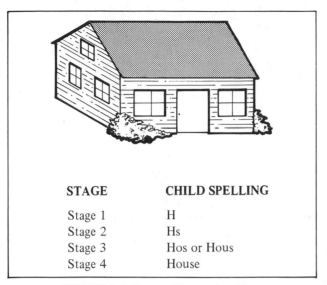

STAGE	CHILD SPELLING
Stage 1	H
Stage 2	Hs
Stage 3	Hos or Hous
Stage 4	House

FIGURE 1–7 Stages of invented spelling

FIGURE 1–8 Example of second stage in spelling development: "Claire" is spelled "Clre."

Figure 1–9 outlines an overall look at the spelling program, including objectives for the child and for the teacher and indications of readiness for spelling.

Words to be Taught in Spelling. The right words for each child will depend upon three things: (1) number of

Objectives for the Child

Learn to spell functional words.
Understand various meanings of words.
Desire awareness of correct and incorrect spelling.
Develop own method of self-diagnosis and study.
Develop habit of looking up doubtful words.

Objectives for the Teacher

Plan a program through diagnostic study that will adapt to individual needs.
Stimulate interest in purposeful writing.
Emphasize correct pronunciation, meaning(s), and use of phonics.
Develop generalizations with the children (not memorization of rules).
Promote good attitudes toward spelling.
Develop independence in all phases of work.
Emphasize the importance of correct spelling.

Readiness for Spelling

Words must be in the child's listening and speaking vocabulary. In addition, these abilities must be present:

- Visual discrimination (dime–dine).
- Auditory discrimination (bear–hair).
- Eye–hand coordination.
- Ability to write capital and small letters.

FIGURE 1–9 A look at the spelling program

words a child can learn according to level of ability, (2) words the child finds interesting and useful, and (3) use of a basal speller as a springboard for a more enriched program.

Common words should be taught first as they tend to have less syllables. Also, many of the less commonly used words have base words that are themselves common words. For example: ship–shipment, dark–darkness.

Also keep in mind words that can be used in composing for special events. For example, "witch" and "Halloween" are hard words to spell but pertain to a holiday of great interest to children. Thus, they should be taught.

Teaching Each Child How to Spell. All children may not need to go through all of the steps shown in Figure 1–10, but each teacher should be aware of these steps. As indicated, the child needs to understand the meaning of the word and to be able to read the word. Encouraging children to check their own work, as soon

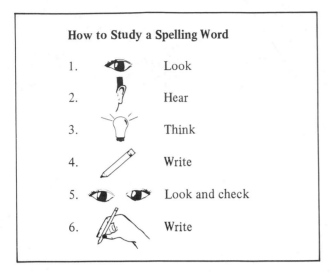

How to Study a Spelling Word

1. Look
2. Hear
3. Think
4. Write
5. Look and check
6. Write

FIGURE 1–10   How to study a spelling word

as they are capable of this, is also important in teaching spelling.

RECEPTIVE SPEECH: LISTENING

Developing effective listening skills deserves a prominent position in language arts instruction in the early elementary grades. The importance of oral communication devices such as the telephone, television, radio, and tape recorder increases the need for listening competency. An inordinately large portion of the children's school day, as well as their leisure time, makes demands on listening skills. They listen in school and out of school. Children listen for directions, for information and knowledge, for acquisition of speaking vocabulary, for enunciation and inflection patterns, and for entertainment. Young children with limited ability in reading are particularly dependent on listening.

Listening is *not* synonymous with hearing, although hearing is essential to the skill. Genuine listening also includes recognizing, interpreting, and responding in some way to that which is heard. Listening can be defined as purposeful hearing, or hearing with understanding.

Children vary widely in their ability to listen. Their previous experiences, auditory acuity, general intelligence, vocabulary, and the manner in which people have listened to them are all factors related to this language skill.

Basic Listening Skills

Recognizing sounds
Hearing and repeating sound sequences
Practicing beginning sounds of words
Identifying and grouping objects beginning with the same sound
Hearing rhyming sounds and matching rhyming objects
Identifying familiar sounds
Recognizing right and left hands
Following directions
Following the sequence of action in a story

FIGURE 1–11   Development of listening skills in the primary grades

Children develop some listening skills before they begin elementary school. Further growth and development of listening is more likely to take place in elementary school with systematic instruction than if left to chance. Learning to listen is a prerequisite to listening to learn. A major task of the elementary school is to help children gain competence in this important language skill. Figure 1–11 summarizes the basic listening skills commonly taught in the early elementary grades.

Remember, there are several types of listening that young children need to develop: (1) *passive or marginal listening*—when a child is engrossed in one activity but listens just enough to be aware of what is going on; (2) *appreciative listening*—when the child enjoys a story, a poem, a recording; (3) *attentive listening*—when the child is given directions or announcements and must pay full attention; and (4) *analytical listening*—when the child analyzes what he hears in terms of his own experiences (one may hear the child as he ponders, "I wonder why?").

Teaching Strategies to Encourage Listening
- Since young children are easily distracted and have short attention spans, plan to be flexible and adjust activities so that young children's ability to pay attention will be enhanced without undue pressure. For example, plan the length of stories, recordings, music, and other class periods to suit the children's ability to pay attention. Remember, shorter is always better than too long!

- Vary the way you present a story, a lesson, or any activity. Use attractive materials, pictures, bright colors, favorite cartoon characters, and similar attention getters.
- Permit wriggling and twisting. It takes constant conscious effort on the part of a little child to hold the body still, and just having to do so may therefore be distracting. In other words, a young child may be so conscious of having to sit still that he can't follow anything that's going on around him.
- Avoid such statements as, "We sit up straight with our feet on the floor." There are many finger plays and songs which appropriately and pleasantly convey such directives. For example:

     Open, shut them.
     Open, shut them.
     Give a little clap.
     Open, shut them.
     Open, shut them.
     Fold them in your lap.

  Then immediately begin the story or presentation.
- Arrange the physical environment so that children are comfortable, and outside noises and interferences are at a minimum.
- To show the child that listening is important, don't repeat explanations. Make activities so interesting that children will want to listen and will miss something if they don't. Speak in a moderate voice; don't try to talk above noises in the room.
- Don't talk too much. Some teachers are guilty of talking on and on. Consequently their voices become monotonous and children will usually tune them out.
- Allow time for children to listen. For example, say, "Boys and girls," pause, and then proceed. Also allow children the opportunity to listen to their own voices in activities such as the ones suggested later in this unit.
- Set a good example yourself. One of the best ways to let a child know listening is important is to be a good listener. Don't become so bogged down in other things that you give an absentminded reply to a child. If a chore is pressing, let someone else help the child; however, the best approach is to leave the chore until you find out what the child wants to say.
- Create a relaxed, happy atmosphere. A child who is happy and free from emotional strain can listen more easily than a tense, hostile, or fearful child.

Center Function and Goals

Listening is a necessary part of group living. Listening skills need to be developed for effective group functioning. The acquisition of listening skills is evidenced by the child's ability to:

- Follow oral directions.
- Sit quietly for short periods.
- Follow a sequence of ideas.
- Wait to comment on questions.
- Watch the speaker.

Participation in listening experiences improves the child's ability to:

- Give others a chance to talk.
- Listen without interrupting.
- Discriminate between sounds.
- Listen for longer periods of time.
- Use different sentence patterns.

Materials and Equipment

Record player and records
Tape recorder (regular or cassette) and tapes
Film-loop projector and film loops
Television
Radio
Walkie-talkie
Dukane projector and filmstrips
Camera and film
Slide viewer and slides
Earphones and jacks
Film projector and films
Overhead projector and transparencies (blank and prepared)
Programmed materials
Pictures

FIGURE 1-12 Sample listening center

- Help children develop an awareness of sounds: a clock ticking, a horn blowing, the freezer motor running, traffic, or even frogs croaking. A good technique is to have the children close their eyes and then identify and describe what they hear. If they can't name the sounds, ask them whether the sound was loud, soft, sharp, close or far away, etc.

FIGURE 1–13   A listening center is a special place to practice listening skills.

FIGURE 1–14   Learning about sounds, sometimes called phonics, is part of the early elementary language arts program. Art activities are good experiences to include in the listening center.

- To be sure there is a special place just for these and other listening activities, create a listening center in the room. The objectives of such a center and the materials needed are described in Figure 1–12.

Activities to Encourage Listening. The following activities will help develop listening skills. More activities are given at the end of this unit.

Calling Attention to the Listening Process
- Have children close their eyes and try to identify another child by listening to him speak.
- Have children close their eyes and listen for a number of seconds. Ask them to name the sounds they heard.
- Read aloud a selection and ask the children to listen for and count the occurrences of a particular word such as "go" or "move."
- Play a sound effects recording and ask students to identify the sounds.
- Tap a rhythm pattern and have the students repeat it. Begin with simple ones and work up to the point each hand taps a different rhythm.
- Have students close their eyes. Drop a number of objects on a desk and ask that the objects be identified according to their sounds.

Developing Skills in Following Directions
- Play "Simon Says."
- Have students listen to and repeat directions for getting to a specific destination.
- Use art activities which include directions for folding and cutting paper.
- Read a paragraph with several directions in it and ask the child to follow them.
- Use prepared worksheets where students must follow such directions as: circle, underline, cross out, etc.
- Read directions for a science experiment and have the students follow them.

Using Contextual Clues
- Use riddles. For example: I am little. I am yellow. I say Quack, Quack. What am I?
- Read sentences aloud, omitting certain words and asking the children to supply them.
- Build sentences by having each child add one or two words. Stories may be built in the same manner. The object of the game is for each child to add something and not let the story end with him.

A.

B.

C.

D.

FIGURE 1–15 The children's book *Frosty the Snowman* had very different effects on four children who heard it. (a) Frosty obviously is the most important feature of this child's drawing. (b) Frosty and the little boy share the focus of this child's drawing. (c) Frosty becomes part of a Christmas scene in this child's creative drawing. (d) The sheer joy of snow is what this child chose to draw after the Frosty story.

- Read aloud open-ended sentences for the children to complete. For example: My dad and I planned to go to the circus yesterday, but ____.

Using Sensory Imagery
- Read aloud short paragraphs which compare people, places, or events. Then have the children recall from memory similarities and differences between them.
- Read aloud sentences which appeal to one or more of the senses. Have students categorize each sentence under the appropriate sense. For example: The smell of bacon frying was all I needed to pull me out of bed.

- Read aloud a poem and have the students draw a picture of the character. For example: "Pirate Don Durk of Dowdee" by Mildred Plew Meigs (in Anderson, 1964).

RECEPTIVE SPEECH: READING

While language arts includes many skills, what comes to mind most frequently when the term is used is simply "reading."

A famous psychiatrist, Bruno Bettelheim, was interviewed about his views of reading in the early school years, as follows (Bettelheim, 1981):

Hall: So reading is not portrayed as part of life.

Bettelheim: Not at all.   So why learn to read? Nor do readers ever show children at school. They're always playing.   Life in these books is nothing but a succession of pleasurable activities on the shallowest level.   And there are no real emotions in the readers. Nobody is angry. Nobody has a fight. Nobody suffers.

Hall: How about the way children think of themselves?

Bettelheim: Well, mostly children think that those who wrote the textbooks and those who teach them to read believe that they're dumbbells. Look at this book.   Here are Mark and Janet. They are the same age and have the same parents. They must be either fraternal twins or adopted, or perhaps the children of different marriages.   These children are the main characters in an entire series of readers, yet such an important issue is never mentioned; our children are treated like idiots who would not wonder about it.   That's my point. Reading should stimulate thinking.   And there we get to the root of the problem: children are not taken seriously.

Early childhood teachers must take children seriously. And this is especially important in the area of reading skills.

Reading, like each of the other areas of language (speaking, writing, composing, and listening), has its own pattern of development and series of related skills. And skill in reading is not always directly related to skill in the other aspects of language development.   Thus it is unfair to assume that a five-year-old is "ready" to read because of rapid speech development. It is just as unfair to expect that all children are ready for reading instruction simply because they are all the same age or grade level. The process of actual reading instruction is beyond the scope of this unit. Our focus here is on the development of *basic* reading skills.

Beginning to Read.   Once children have developed visual discrimination and letter recognition, they are able to learn simple words.   At this point children often learn spontaneously to read the words that they see around them.   This is called simple word recognition or "sight" vocabulary.   For example, they begin to recognize the names of their favorite television shows, not by sounding out the words, but by simple recall and association of the word with the program.   They learn to read the name of their favorite restaurant. They see many other words, such as "STOP" and "WALK," on street signs. By pointing out these familiar signs to young children and reading what they say, you will help increase children's sight vocabulary.

Activities to Encourage Reading. Here are some other activities to develop sight vocabulary.   Additional activities will be found at the end of the unit.

• Choose four or five words that name objects around the classroom, such as door, wall, clock, floor, chair, table.   Print each word on a plain index card or on a 3″ × 4″ strip of plain paper.   Tape each card to the object it names. When children become familiar with these words, add new ones.

• To help develop both sight vocabulary and visual discrimination (matching, too) print the same words on a second set of cards.   Give the word cards to a child, and ask him to find the words that look the same.   You may want to give the child some tape so that he can tape the word cards next to the ones you have put up.   As a child learns the words, mix up the cards and say: "Find the one that says wall." Gradually begin to add new words.

• As children begin to learn words, place the words on vocabulary cards.   Use different sizes, shapes, and colors of paper and four different letter sizes to help ensure that the words will be recognized wherever they are found.   This is a good way to combine word and shape recognition, too.

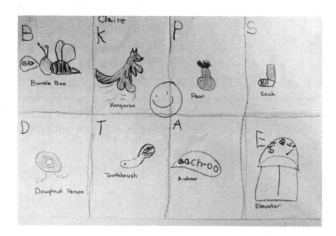

FIGURE 1–16 Beginning sound recognition is one of the first steps to reading.

FIGURE 1–17 An effective beginning word recognition activity is to label the child's pictures.

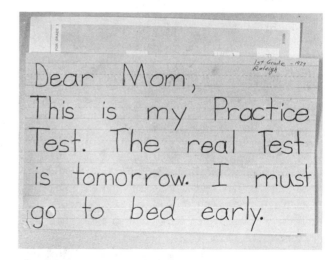

FIGURE 1–18 Capitalize on announcements to teach words in a meaningful context. Writing a note to parents emphasizes the use of writing as a means of communicating important things.

- Reading also involves the ability to hear different sounds, termed "auditory discrimination." To help children develop auditory skills for reading, use rhyming words. Ask if any of the words the child has learned to read rhyme with each other or with other words the child may know: for example, door–floor, chair–bear. Play a guessing game: "I am thinking of something that rhymes with lamp. You lick it and put it on a letter. What is it?"

- When children can hear rhyming words, help them listen to the beginning sounds of words. For example, say the word "table," emphasizing the *t* sound at the beginning. Ask the child to name any other words that start with the same sound as table: for example, tent, tiger, toy. Then go on to another sound.

- Lone Wolf. Make a deck of about 20 index cards with one additional card for the "Lone Wolf." On half the cards print a word. On the remaining cards print the same words, so that all of the cards form pairs except the Lone Wolf. The word on the Lone Wolf card can be changed frequently, thus eliminating the chance for memorization. Deal all of the cards. Each child in turn draws from the person next to him. If he has the card to make a pair, he draws again. The child left with the odd card at the end of the game is the Lone Wolf.

- Record the child's own talking by the use of experience charts. Use words and sentences from the experience charts for matching.

- Provide various media for writing, so the child can get the "feel" of the word. Media such as acetate and felt pens, chalk lap boards, finger paint, and sand can be used.

- Allow children to write labels and captions for objects in the classroom and throughout the school.

- Encourage children to keep a word book of their favorite words. These can be used for alphabetizing, classifying, creative writing, and spelling.
- Capitalize on announcements, birthdays, and thank-you notes to teach words in meaningful context.
- Use partners or child-teachers for sight vocabulary drill.

THE LEARNING ENVIRONMENT FOR LANGUAGE ARTS

Finally, it is not enough to understand the skills of language that need to be developed in the early elementary grades. Just as important is the environment in which these learnings take place. Careful planning of the environment is essential to the success of the language arts program. The following basic characteristics need to be kept in mind.

- *Flexibility* is the key.
- Many methods and techniques are used.
- Schedules utilize large blocks of time.
- There is opportunity for coordination among the various areas of study.
- The supply of materials is ample and diverse enough to satisfy differences in children's interests and rates of growth.
- The room is an active, busy laboratory with pupils moving purposefully about, carrying out plans, seeking ideas of their peers, discussing what they find, and coming to increased understandings.
- Interest centers and work areas in the room foster such activities.
- There are times when the teacher and the whole class are working together. There is also time for the teacher to work with small groups of pupils or individuals, for small groups of pupils to work by themselves, and for individuals to work alone.
- It is not an "as quiet as a mouse" room nor are the desks and chairs in straight rows. Furniture is arranged to facilitate movement and a variety of activities. There is movement and a hum of purposeful activity.
- Provision is made for keeping comprehensive records on each child to be used in examining and analyzing needs as well as progress.

The physical organization of classroom instruction is a vital part of providing for effective learning. There are general essentials to consider before making decisions regarding types of centers to include and the kinds of materials to select for each center. A good learning environment requires establishment of routines with the children, provision of adequate supplies and equipment, freedom for movement, and places as well as times for evaluation, conferences, and sharing. The following checklist is offered as a guide to setting up a functional room:

- Quiet areas arranged together for reading, writing, and listening.
- Noisier activities together for manipulative use.
- Health factors involving lighting, ventilation, and cleanliness considered.
- Equipment and materials in best light for close eye work.
- Wide selection of materials to meet interests and capabilities.
- Materials accessible for pupil responsibility.
- Flexibility in arrangement, with seating in clusters.
- Audio-visual aids, drama props, games, and other devices available.
- Some centers are more permanent than others.
- Appropriate nooks for times when children need to be alone.
- Classroom purposefully reflecting interests and activities of children.

SUMMARY

Language arts is generally divided into two components: expressive language and receptive language. Expressive language includes speaking and writing. Receptive language includes the skills of listening and reading. Writing skills include the forming of letters as well as composing skills.

In planning for language arts experiences in the early elementary years, young children should not be mistaken for miniature elementary students needing only a "watered-down" elementary program. Instead, language arts experiences in the early elementary years must be right for the developmental level of the children in the program. Some children may be ready to read, some may be just beginning to recognize letters or their own names, and others may be anywhere in between.

To meet the developmental needs of young children, language arts in the early elementary years must provide children with opportunities to:

- Use language freely and effectively based on effective speech models.
- Expand their vocabularies through personal experiences.
- Listen to interesting poems and stories in order to develop good listening habits.
- Read at their own developmental level.
- Develop writing skill based upon personal language experiences.

FIGURE 1-19 Children's books are a natural part of the elementary language arts program.

LEARNING ACTIVITIES

A. Plan, implement, and evaluate at least two activities for each of the main areas of language development discussed in this unit. Discuss your results with members of your class.

B. Role play a story hour where the teacher encourages children to verbalize as fully as possible. Use the guidelines provided in this unit for encouraging speech in your role playing.

C. Observe a first grade classroom. Keep a record of the commands, monologues, and closed-type questions a teacher uses in one hour. For the next hour keep a record of the open-ended questions, conversation-encouraging statements, and so on. Compare your two observations.

D. Use one of the techniques for encouraging speech with young children. Discuss the results of your use of the technique. What would you do differently next time?

E. Take a tape recorder with you to a first, second, or third grade room. Record the story time or group reading time. Analyze the recorded session for speech-encouraging examples.

F. Obtain samples of writing from first and second grade youngsters. Indicate age on each sample. Bring these samples into class. Compare all the first and second graders. Note the differences in letter formation, size of letters, and any other noticeable differences.

G. Use one of the suggested activities to encourage children's composing. Bring in the children's sentences and read them aloud to the class.

H. Play one of the suggested spelling games. Evaluate the activity and share your results with the class.

I. Using a school supply catalog, choose at least three items you would purchase for a listening center. Explain why you choose the item and the purpose the item will serve.

J. Design on paper a language arts center for a first, second, and third grade. What differences would there be between grade levels and why? What specific equipment would you include in your center? Why?

ACTIVITIES FOR CHILDREN

Speaking

A. *Different Ways of Saying Things.* Students will enjoy experimenting with different ways of saying the same words or sentences. Let them try saying the following sentences first *laughingly,* then *sadly,* and last *angrily:*

"Am I going with you?"

"It just doesn't seem to fit."

B. *Pantomime.* Select a picture that might bring out certain emotions. Have the students explain how they would feel if they were one of the children in the picture.

C. *Phone Houses.* It is important for children to remember their address and telephone number. But they will need lots of practice to get all those words and numbers in the right order. Draw a simple house on a large piece of paper, and have the child color in the details. Print the child's address on the house with a dark crayon or a felt-tip pen. Then draw a large telephone, have the child color it, and fill in the child's telephone number. Tape the pictures in a place where the child will see them every day and go over them with the child until he learns them.

D. *Moving to the Sound of Your Whole Name* (Elemenrary level). The children are seated. Call on one child at a time at first to demonstrate. The other children can be thinking.

1. Can you identify the number of parts (syllables) in your whole name (first and last)?

2. Can you clap your hands to the parts of your first and last name?

3. Can you step in place to the parts of your first and last name, taking one step for each syllable?

4. Can you jump around the room, one jump for every syllable of your name?

E. *Learning Appreciation for Our Language.*

1. Have the children say the word "*wiggle,*" then say several words that rhyme with "*wiggle.*" Have them say the word "*slurp,*" then think of several words that rhyme with "*slurp.*"

2. Take a word such as "*man*" and see how many "funny" rhymes can be made with it:

A funny old man

_____

_____

3. Form two teams. Have one team give a word and the other team respond with a rhyming word.

4. Read several rhyming words and one that does not and have the children respond to the one word which does not rhyme.

5. Have students make up jingles to read to the class. Have other students identify the rhyming words.

6. Read aloud a series of nonsense syllables and have the students repeat them. (Examples for this activity may be found in *The Complete Nonsense of Edward Lear.*)

F. *Making a Movie.* Have children make pictures to illustrate a story they have read. Join the pictures to form a scroll, and attach the scroll to dowel rods. Then tape record the story, giving each child a portion of the story to read. Play the tape and turn the scroll to give the movie effect. It's fun to choose a story related to a special day or event and to show the movie to another class. For example: a story about Lincoln for Lincoln's birthday.

G. *Taping the Child's Message*

1. Equipment: A tape recorder and tapes.

2. Procedure: Say, "Today each of you will get to have your voice recorded on the tape recorder. I will tell you a message; then you repeat it into the tape recorder."

Stand by the tape recorder. Tell the child the sentence. Then have the child repeat the sentence into the tape recorder. Play back the sentences so the child can hear himself.

Start with a three-word phrase and increase to 10- or 12-word sentences.

If you cannot understand the child's taped utterance, model the sentence again, this time on tape. Have the child listen to you on tape. Then have the child repeat the sentence.

3. Later, as children get used to taping their voices, let them tape their own "special" messages on the recorder.

H. *Slide Story*

1. Equipment: A filmstrip projector and films telling simple stories.

2. Procedure: Show a short story of 15 to 20 frames. Talk about it while you show it.

Then reshow the story one frame at a time; have the children tell the story this time. Have one child tell about each frame. You are striving for spontaneous language so accept what the child says; reinforce him, and, if appropriate, expand his utternace.

3. Variation: Try having the children tell about the story the first time through without your telling the story first.

I. *Catalog Hunt*
   1. Equipment: A catalog or books with pictures of the same things or of plural objects (for example, two cats, three dogs) up to five.
   2. Procedure: Say, "Today I would like you to look for pictures of _____ for me. When you find a picture, bring it to me and tell me how many _____ are in the picture." Or say, "Everyone look for a picture of two _____. When you find it, bring it to me and tell me what you have."

   When a child brings a picture, he should say: two _____s. If he does not use the *s,* model it and have him repeat what you say. Reinforce the child when he uses plurals.

J. *Finding Sequence*
   1. Read aloud a story and have the children retell the events in the order in which they occurred.
   2. Read a selection in which there is a clear sequence of events; leave out the ending. Ask the children to predict what might happen next.
   3. Scramble the events in a story. Read them aloud and ask the children to rearrange them.

Handwriting

A. Collect samples of children's handwriting for children to examine—from poor to good. Provide examples of good and poor spacing, slant, size, strokes, and shape.
B. Devise individual diagnostic checkoff sheets.
C. Provide charts in the room to remind children of correct form.
D. Set up "Handwriting Clinics." Have "Doctors of Handwriting" diagnose weaknesses in papers of themselves and their classmates.
E. Arrange three pockets for papers to be filed by individuals: "In a Hurry," "Just So-So," "My Best."
F. Keep dated samples for frequent evaluations.

G. Place children's papers on the bulletin board. Have them write more legible papers to replace them.
H. Observe pupils during writing period to determine whether the mechanics of handwriting are becoming automatic.
I. Make class address books.
J. Make class autograph books.
K. Study the history of handwriting.
L. Write compositions about handwriting.
M. Have resource people come in to talk about the importance of handwriting.
N. Write messages in code.
O. Use an opaque projector to show anonymous samples of handwriting to critique.
P. Use colored chalk to illustrate direction or sequence of strokes.
Q. Use acetate overlays to improve letter formation.

Composing

A. *Writing Sentences.* Make a list of the kinds of sentences to be written. For example:
   Write a sentence about a friend.
   Write a sentence naming your city and state.
   Write a sentence about your favorite book.
   Ask the children to use dark pencils and unlined white paper in order that transparencies of their sentences can be made. Place sentences made by the children on the overhead and evaluate them. For example: Johnny used a capital letter on the word "Raleigh." Why?
B. *Other Motivators for Writing*
   1. Specific topics.
   2. Invented circumstances.
   3. Nonsense titles.
   4. Beginning sentences.
   5. Beginning paragraphs.
   6. Random phrases.
   7. Familiar experiences.
   8. Specific objects (baby shoes, trophy, clock, suitcase).
   9. Picture collections.
   10. Comic strips without narration.
   11. Book covers.
   12. Various open themes (descriptions, dialogue, narration, argument and persuasion, short stories, poetry, and emotions).

C. *Confused Sentences.* Motivate interest in sentences by reading sentences that are funny because they are incomplete, have modifiers in the wrong place, or use inappropriate descriptive words. Have the children present skits or cartoons illustrating confused sentences.

D. *Sequence.* Let each child write directions for a very simple activity such as making a peanut butter sandwich. Then have them exchange papers and have one read how to make the sandwich as the other makes the sandwich following those directions.

Spelling

A. *Baseball Game.* Form two teams. On the floor, arrange three bases and home plate. As a child comes to bat for his team, give him three words to spell. If he spells all three correctly, he has made a hit and advances to base. If he misses one of the words he is out and has to wait for another turn. When a runner has been advanced to home plate by his teammates, he scores a run. Emphasize the fact that if a child tells another how to spell his word, that is an automatic out for his side.

B. *Eraso.* Children take turns writing words to be practiced on the board. A child is chosen to erase one of the words while the other children cover their eyes. The children uncover their eyes and tell what word was erased and how it was spelled.

C. *Fishing.* A tabletop serves as a fish pond. The children cut out paper fish and write spelling words on one side. They place the fish, words down, on the table. A game warden is chosen. He calls on children to come up and "fish for a word." The child gives the fish to the warden, who calls out the word and has the "fisherman" spell it. If the child spells the word correctly, then that is his fish; if not, the fish goes back in the pond.
Variation: Instead of fish, a fish pond, and a game warden, you could have cookies, a cookie jar, and a cook.

D. *The Orange Spelling Tree*
   1. Cut an outline of a large tree from green or brown construction paper. Paste or pin the tree to a bright blue background on a bulletin board or flannel board.
   2. Cut orange paper circles (4″ in diameter). Cut green leaves (3″ X 1½″).

3. Cut green and orange strips (1″ X 7″). Then cut them in half up to 6½″. Cut two parallel slits 1″ from the center bottom of each paper orange and leaf. Thread one strip through each orange and leaf.
4. With heavy black crayon print a spelling word on each orange and each leaf.
5. Each pupil picks an orange or a leaf, takes it to his seat, and uses the word in a written sentence. The completed sentences are read aloud. If a sentence is well written, the pupil keeps the orange or leaf as a bookmark. If the sentence is poorly constructed, the orange or leaf is returned to the tree for another chance later.

E. *Other Spelling Activities*
   1. Arrange words in alphabetical order.
   2. Make a spelling design with word cards.
   3. Write interesting sentences, stories, or riddles using spelling words.
   4. Divide words into syllables, emphasizing correct pronunciation.
   5. Work or construct a crossword puzzle.
   6. Write definitions.
   7. Make illustrations.
   8. Choose letters from a letter box and form spelling words.
   9. Work with spelling words on the chalk board.
   10. Write a homonym, synonym, antonym, or a rhyming word with a spelling word.
   11. Classify spelling words according to long or short vowels, number of syllables, or generalizations being taught at the time.

Listening

A. *Analyzing Moods and Emotions*
   1. Read aloud short selections and have students write down the words which helped to create the mood.
   2. Record conversations in which speakers change their moods. After playing a recording, ask students to make one-word comments to identify the mood. For example: angry, happy, apologetic, concerned.

B. *Knock-Knock.* In this game one child sits with his back to the class and his eyes closed. Another child knocks on the sitter's chair. The sitter asks "Who's there?" The other child answers, "It is I." The sitter must then identify him and tell how he knew. (The child will often answer that he listened to hear where the footsteps came from, or heard some specific tone quality.) After the children are well acquainted with one another's voices, this game can be varied by having them pitch their voices lower or higher. They also enjoy disguising their voices by imitating some animal.

C. *Who Said It* (variation of Knock-Knock). Four or five children stand in front of the classroom. The rest of the class sits with backs to them. One child is selected to say something such as "Hello" or "Good Morning," etc. Individuals in the class must identify the speaker. The game continues until all are identified. Then each child is touched again, but this time he must disguise his voice. When someone guesses him, he trades places with the guesser.

D. *Yes or No*. The children sit informally before the teacher with their hands folded in their laps. The teacher makes true and false statements such as "A car can eat hay," "A duck can climb a tree," "A cat can chase a mouse." If the statement is true the children keep their hands in their laps, but if it is false they raise their hands, still folded, over their heads. To keep this game going with very young children, the teacher should be "it."

E. *Theodora Thank-You*
   1. Equipment: A tape recorder and tape with "Thank you" recorded on it in a variety of pitches and funny, exaggerated ways approximately 20 times; a doll, puppet, or picture to be introduced to children as "Theodora Thank-You"; some blocks.
   2. Procedure: Have children sit around a table or on the floor in a circle. Place blocks in the center of circle or table. Sit with the recorder on your lap and introduce Theodora by saying, "This is Theodora Thank-You. She is very polite. She would like for you to follow my directions. Each time you do, she will have something to say to you." Giving each child a turn, direct him to put a block somewhere. Example: "John, put a block *on* the floor." "Bill give a block to Sue." When a direction is followed, press the recorder and have Theodora thank the child.
   3. Variations:
      a. Have the children give simple directions to each other. Children should be trained in use of the tape recorder so they can use it independently.
      b. Have oaktag block patterns prepared for children to use independently. The child follows directions by covering the original pattern of squares with blocks of the same dimensions.

F. *My Head Is a Swing*. Children and teacher chant, "My head is a swing and it swings and swings and swings" as they swing their heads up and down, side to side, around and around, allowing the head to fall as far as possible each time. They continue to swing other body parts as they chant:
   "My arm is a swing. . .
   "Both arms are swings. . .
   "My trunk is a swing. . .
   "My leg is a swing. . .
They travel backward and forward and sideways as they continue to swing various body parts. As they swing the arms upward, they allow the body to move upward in a leap or jump. The body is a part of every swing. Teacher and children list things that swing, such as an elephant's trunk, a train signal, a playground swing, and the pendulum of a clock. Children work with a partner or in groups as they show with their own swing patterns the idea of something that swings.

G. *Flying*
   1. Procedure: The children stand either beside their desks or in an open area of the classroom. The leader stands in front of the group and says, "The sparrow is flying." At the same time, the leader moves his arms rapidly up and down. The other children move their arms up and down in response. Each succeeding time the leader changes the name of the bird; for instance, "The robin is flying." If the leader names any animal that does not fly, the children must not move their arms even though the leader does. When a child moves his arms at the wrong time, he takes his seat. The last child standing wins the game.

2. Variations:
   a. The children walk around the room, moving their arms in a flying motion, but stop when something other than a bird is named.
   b. The children move their arms in a swimming motion and the names of fish are substituted for the names of birds. The leader would say, for instance, "The minnow is swimming."
   c. Use other large categories for this game.

Reading

Alphabet Recognition

A. *Discrimination Relay*
   1. Equipment: Index cards.
   2. Procedure: Sometimes children have trouble discriminating between various letters of the alphabet. For example, the letters *b* and *d*. In this case, write the letter *b* on one side of a card and *d* on the other side. Form the children into three or four teams and give a card to each team. Position the card holders 30 to 40 feet in front of each squad. The children will hold the cards behind their backs. When the first squad members leave the starting line, the card is held in front. The students must run around the letter the way it is "looking." The squad that finishes first wins. Example: *b*—run around to the right, *d*—run around to the left; *m*—run around the child two times, *n*—run around the child once; *r*—run half way around the child and back; *h*—run all the way around the child with one hand in the air.
   3. Variations: Any number of skills may be used with these activities. For example: walking, running, hopping, skipping rope, jumping, animal walks, ball handling skills, and obstacle courses.

B. *Toss and Answer*
   1. Equipment: Two wastebaskets, a set of alphabet consonant cards, a set of basic word cards taken from the reading text's vocabulary.
   2. Procedure: Place a set of alphabet consonant cards in each wastebasket, and place the wastebaskets on the floor at a specified distance from two teams of children. The first child tosses a beanbag into the basket. If the beanbag lands in the basket, the child takes a card from the basket.

If he can think of a word that begins (or ends, as the teacher specifies) with that letter, his team gets a point, and it's the other team's turn to toss the bean bag. If the child cannot name a word correctly, he can use the stack of word cards to help him. Each child has two chances to toss the beanbag into the basket.

C. *Snail Jump.* Using masking tape, chalk, or paint on oil cloth or the floor to make a large snail. Write letters in each section of the snail, using both small and capital letters. Ask the children:

- Can you hop on your left foot on all the letters, naming each letter?
- Can you jump on your right foot on all the letters, giving a word beginning with each letter?
- Can you hop on every other letter on the snail?

D. *Alphabet Jump*
   1. Equipment: Alphabet cards, beanbag, blackboard or additional sets of alphabet flash cards.
   2. Procedure: Divide the class into two teams. Scatter one set of alphabet cards in one area of the floor in random order, an identical set in another area. Each team forms a line. A member of the opposing team writes a letter of the alphabet on the board. The first child in line finds that letter and jumps on it. He then goes to the end of the line. Play continues with another letter being written and erased. When the original player is first in line again, play is over. The team finishing first wins.
   3. Variations: Use the same procedure but have the opposing team member hold up a letter or flash card, count to three, and then hide the card behind his back.

E. *Alphabet Toss.* The children stand in a circle, and one child tosses a ball or a beanbag to any other child and calls out a word such as "ball." The child must then name another word beginning with the letter *B* before the hand of the clock makes one revolution (or before a kitchen timer goes off).

F. *Alphabet Hop.* Draw a hopscotch pattern on the playground or on the classroom floor with chalk. Put a familiar consonant in each section. As the child hops onto a letter, he must say a word that begins with the same letter. The next child does the same but must use different words. If a word is repeated, the child loses that turn.

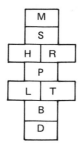

Word Recognition
A. *Jumbled Word*

1. Procedure: Prepare a set of cards, each containing a picture and jumbled letters of the corresponding word. Cover the cards with clear contact paper. Prepare a stencil so that the child can write down his answers by the corresponding numbers. The child will unscramble each word and write down the answers.

2. Variations: The child may write the correct word directly on the card with a washable marker or use letter cards to form the words.

B. *Hang-Up Relay*

1. Equipment: Write vocabulary or spelling words on 3″ X 5″ index cards. Make two sets of 2″ X 3″ alphabet cards and punch holes in the tops. Cut two 2″ X 15″ boards out of tri-wall, wood, or pressed board. Fasten a cup hook every 2″ near the top of the boards.

2. Procedure: Divide the class into two teams. Hold up a "stimulus card"; for example, "house." One child from each team selects the beginning letter from the alphabet cards and places it on the first hook on the left of his team's board. The relay

continues with other team members adding letters to complete the word.

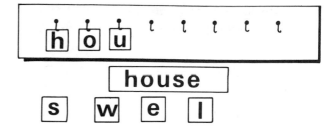

C. *Catch Words*

1. Equipment: A whiffle ball for every two children and small pieces of paper with reading words on them.

2. Procedure: Roll the pieces of paper and place them in the holes of a whiffle ball. Two children stand opposite each other and toss the ball between them. The teacher or another child gives a signal at intervals, perhaps by ringing a bell. The child with the ball removes a piece of paper and reads the word. The child receives one point for reading the word correctly. The child with the most points wins.

D. *Matching Card Game.*
A set of printed word cards is used. Each word should occur on four cards. The players are each dealt three or five cards, and five cards are placed face up on the table. If the first child to play has a card in his hand marked "horse" and there is a "horse" card on the table, he may expose his card, pronounce the word, and place the two "horse" cards face up in front of him. If he does not have a card which matches any of the exposed cards on the table, he must discard one of his own cards, and draw another from the pack. If he has a matching card, but cannot pronounce it, he places it on top of the card on the table which it matches and draws a card from the pack. If a child can make more than one match at a time, he may do so. Drawing a card from the pack ends his play. The second player follows the procedure of the first, except that he may match with and pronounce any cards face up on the table and take them. For example, if the first player has taken "horse," and the second player has a "horse" card, he may take the two cards in front of the first

player. Another player possessing the fourth "horse" card may in turn claim the three "horse" cards already collected. The same procedure is followed with respect to the pairs or triplets of cards that collect in the center of the table because of failure on the player's part to pronounce them. When the pack of cards is exhausted, the players continue as before, except that they do not draw. Thus the hands are soon played and the game is over. The player with the most cards before him has won.

UNIT REVIEW

1. List the two main areas of language arts and the skills involved in each.
2. Describe how to arrange a room so that it is conducive to a good language arts program. Describe the characteristics of a good language arts program.
3. What is the main way a child learns to speak? List ways a teacher can encourage the growth of speech skill.
4. List some strategies to encourage a child to listen.
5. What are the various skills involved in writing (forming letters)? What are some things to avoid in teaching children how to write?
6. Describe some ways to encourage children to compose, including activities.
7. Outline the basic sequence in the development of composing skill. Give at least two examples of activities for each stage of composing.
8. What are the stages of invented spelling? Give an example for each stage.
9. How can you know which words to teach children? How do you go about teaching a child spelling? Give examples of activities in your reply.
10. What are some guidelines for encouraging good listening skills?
11. What is "sight" vocabulary and how can you help a child's growth in this area? Include examples of games.

ADDITIONAL READINGS

Applegate, Mauree. *Freeing Children to Write.* New York: Harper and Row, 1963.

Bettelheim, Bruno. "Our Children are Treated Like Idiots." *Psychology Today.* July, 1981.

Language Arts

Anderson, P. *Language Arts in Elementary Education.* New York: Macmillan, 1964.

Fox, Sharon E. *The Language Arts—An Integrated Approach.* New York: Holt, Rinehart and Winston, 1983.

Lear, Edward. *The Complete Nonsense of Edward Lear.* New York: Dover, 1951.

Machado, J.M. *Early Childhood Experiences in Language Arts.* New York: Delmar, 1979.

Scott, Louise. *Learning Time With Language Experiences for Young Children.* New York: McGraw-Hill, 1968.

Reading

Lapps, Diane, and Flood, James. *Teaching Reading to Every Child.* New York: Macmillan, 1983.

Lee D.M., and Rubin, J.D. *Children and Language: Reading and Writing, Talking and Listening.* Belmont, Calif.: Wadsworth, 1979.

Unit 2 Language Arts Activities

OBJECTIVES

After studying this unit, you will be able to

- describe at least three activities to use in teaching young children listening skills.
- describe at least three activities to help develop children's speaking skills.
- describe at least three reading activities appropriate for the early elementary grades.
- describe at least three activities for writing (forming letters) and three for composing.

The activities suggested in this unit are by no means complete, but it is hoped that they will get you started in making the language arts program interesting and meaningful for young children.

Since young children in a typical classroom have a wide range of reading and language abilities, you should feel free to adapt activities to the interests, needs, and abilities of each child. To assist you in using these activities, they have been grouped into the same main language arts areas discussed in Unit 1: speaking, listening, reading, and writing, including letter formation and composing.

It is the intent of this unit to encourage you to experiment with these activities in the classroom in order to find out which best suit the youngsters' needs. No specific grade level has been assigned to these activities. The teacher's knowledge of the child will be the basis for any grade designation.

EXPRESSIVE LANGUAGE ACTIVITIES

Speaking. Role playing enables the child to speak about things of high interest, in the protected guise of "someone else." Some examples of role playing are:

- A policeman directing traffic after an accident.
- A forest ranger finding an injured raccoon in the forest.
- A mother losing her child at the fair.
- A child missing the bus.
- An angry father punishing a child.
- A teacher talking to two children who have eaten another child's lunch.
- A child having her first big birthday party.

Story telling can also develop naturally from the children's role playing. Have a child dress as an oldtimer spinning a sea yarn, a witch reviewing her favorite hair-raising experience, an old man or woman recounting earlier days. Ask children to use a check list as they prepare and present a story-telling assignment:

1. Was my story appropriate for the age of the audience?
2. Did I use expression of face and voice?
3. Were the events of my story well planned?
4. Was my voice loud and clear?
5. Did I use simple props or costumes to make my story more interesting?

Use a tape recorder for reluctant readers. Have the child record her story, and later have someone write it down for her. It is her story, and she will practice in order to read it as she said it and as it was written for her. Also have children use the tape recorder for reading to hear actual voice level and pronunciation and to observe speed and breath control. Record special radio plays for the class.

Some children will not talk out their problems. Therefore, try open-ended questions or situations that can be written down. Examples:

- One day in school John took Ken's eraser and wouldn't give it back. What should Ken do?
- John tripped Susan as she carried a tray of paints to the back of the room, and Miss Smith scolded her. Susan's cheeks burned, but the rest of the class laughed. Susan felt it had not been her fault and that she had been scolded unjustly. What should she do?

A poem can motivate discussion or writing about a child's interests or feelings. For example:

I Keep Three Wishes Ready
I keep three wishes ready,
Lest I should chance to meet,
Any day a fairy
Coming down the street.

I'd hate to have to stammer,
Or have to think them out,
For it's very hard to think things up
When a fairy is about.

And I'd hate to lose my wishes
For fairies fly away,
And perhaps I'd never have a chance
On any other day.

So I keep three wishes ready,
Lest I should chance to meet
Any day a fairy
Coming down the street.
                        —Annette Wynne

Have the children either dictate or write their wishes. These wishes can give insight into the child's background. Exciting places to keep the wishes could be:

- On the back of each child's footprint and displayed on a bulletin board.
- On small scrolls scattered around the fairy's castle.

Following are some storytelling ideas.

- Telling stories both real and imaginary to class.
- Beginning a story and letting children add to it as they have ideas.
- Inviting individuals to tell stories by interpreting pictures.
- Asking children to tell stories about their own paintings.
- Helping children see stories in the things that happen around them.
- Forming small groups for "pass-it-on" stories.
- Letting children retell stories they have read.
- Encouraging pupils to dictate original stories, poems, plays, and songs.
- Telling original stories, having children anticipate the events, and incorporating these into the story.

- Playing a game of "Going Fishing" in which pupils choose topics and tell one-minute stories about them.

To encourage conversation:

- Start a Sharing Club in which children share riddles, books, news events, original stories, and poems.
- Establish centers of interest where children can help each other explore, experiment, and find answers to their questions.
- Play a game of "Telephone," in which children learn to take accurate messages.
- Start a discussion by asking, "How did your day begin?"
- For sentence expansion, use sentence strips (see illustration) with one child, partners, or with small groups.

```
look for a lady frog
— — — — — —
croak all day
— — — — — —
hop on a lily pad
— — — — — —

I am a big green frog in a pond.  I will . . . . . . .
```

- For quiet talks, have children choose topics from cards with examples such as: "What A Horrible Day!" "My Big Moment!"
- Stimulate problem solving by asking, "How would you spend _____?"
- Initiate enumeration activities with questions like, "How many different ways does an animal get food?"
- Evoke comparisons by asking such questions as "In what ways are hockey and soccer alike?"
- Begin discussions about specific topics, e.g., encourage youngsters to tell what they are afraid of.

To encourage discussion:

- Ask "What if . . . ?" questions. For example, "What if you were a little green frog in a boy's pocket?"
- Initiate problem solving. For example, "Why are the fish in the aquarium dying?"
- Discuss things children bring to class.
- Plan a trip or activity.

- Have children retell a fairytale from the villain's point of view.
- Use motivating books, records, filmstrips, toys, and animals.
- Speculate on the outcome of a story before reading the conclusion.
- Start discussion clubs on the basis of interests or friendship.
- Have panel discussions.

Handwriting. To help children learn small and large letters make a column of capital letters and a column of lowercase letters on the chalkboard. Using a small group, throw a yarn ball to an individual. The one who catches the ball goes and points to the lowercase and capital for a designated letter.

This activity shows the pupil how to begin correctly and is a pleasant diversion from ordinary practicing. Make an outline of a letter using numbered dots. The child is to write the letter by beginning with the smallest number and progressing to the largest. Upon reaching the largest number, the letter will be complete.

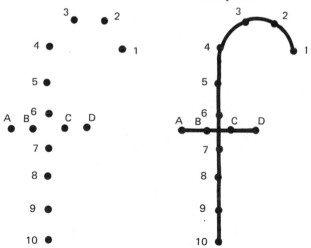

Have the child write a line of a particular letter of the alphabet. Then have her go back and compare the letters she has made with a standard one from a handwriting book or some other model. She is then to circle the one example of her work that best resembles the model. Next, she is to underline the example that least resembles the model and be able to explain what is wrong with it.

List, number, and talk about handwriting rules (every letter must be on the line, etc.). Give a color to each rule. Have the child evaluate her own writing by underlining with the correct color the letter or word that does not conform to the rule.

Have children write words in alphabetical order on numbered lines. For example:

cat   boy   end   an   doll

1. _____
2. _____
3. _____
4. _____
5. _____

Have the child write an identification tag including name, address, and telephone number. She will then compare it to the handwriting book to see which letters and numbers need more practice.

Writing at the chalkboard is a good introduction to writing for most children. The chalkboard provides space for large movements, and affords the writer a clear view of what she is writing. Also, the teacher can easily observe handwriting behavior and provide individual help before errors become habits. Motivation for doing a good job is high and children like to write on the board. If a section of the chalkboard can be reserved for this activity, writing practice during free time is likely to be a popular choice.

Handwriting usually develops in this sequence	Materials for Handwriting
Writing name Labeling pictures Writing simple sentences (from teacher's model) Writing stories and poems (individually and groups) Improving quality and legibility Refining movement Developing individual style	Chalkboard and chalk Unruled newsprint, large crayons and pencils Large chart paper and felt pens or crayons Ruled primary writing paper and large pencils Primary transitional writing paper and regular-size pencils Standard-size notebook paper and pencils or pens

FIGURE 2–1 Sequence of handwriting development and materials needed

Composing

Surprise Box. Make a chart of suggested activities for children to do after they have finished assigned work. Children select an activity and put it in a box called the "Surprise Box." Check and give recognition for extra work. Some possibilities:

- Write a letter to a friend.
- Write a poem or story.
- Write ten compound words.

Sound Pictures. Have children draw pictures to represent sounds, such as: a boy beating a drum, galloping horses, a whistling boy.

Newspaper. Pupils in primary grades enjoy composing a daily newspaper. Each morning devote a half hour to supplying and reading their news. Children copy the best items in manuscript writing and illustrate them. A reporter, chosen for a period of a week, collects news from her room. The objectives of the newspaper are to stimulate interest in reading and to enlarge reading vocabulary. Here is an excerpt:

> Philip brought some coral and a starfish for our science table. Nancy's dog, Tippy, has four new baby puppies. Bobby and Lyle went on a hike to the woods on Saturday.

Winnie the Pooh. One teacher found reading *Winnie the Pooh* motivating to young children. The day after she read Chapter 5 (in which Piglet meets the Heffalump) to her second grade class, she prepared a surprise for them. The children entered the room to find signs hanging from long strings around the room. On the signs were questions like:

- What is a Heffalump?
- Is it fierce?
- Did it come when you whistled?
- Was it fond of pigs at all?
- How did it walk?

These questions were quoted from the book and the children were to answer them in story form. The big question, "How would you trap a Heffalump?" really sparked the imagination of the boys in particular. One child, who had previously written only two- or three-sentence stories, spent nearly a week on this story, ending with a two-page typewritten description of the trapping of a Heffalump.

Beginnings and Endings. Begin a story for the children to complete according to their ideas and abilities. For example:

- I like to . . .
- I like . . .
- We saw . . .
- We went to . . .
- Did you ever . . .
- Did you know that . . .

Or provide an ending for a story:

- . . . and the balloon flew high up in the sky.
- . . . so they all ran home.
- . . . but no one could find it.

What I Thought About It. After children have seen a film or play, or heard a record, let them write about what they thought of it. Let them tell what they liked the best and what they would change if they could.

Nursery Rhymes. Read nursery rhymes to the children. Let the group say them along with you. Have individuals recite rhymes they know.

Dramatize the rhymes.

The children can make individual pictures of the rhymes. These can be cut out and pasted on a mural and a background colored in.

Riddles can be made up about the rhymes. For example, "Who Am I? I'm round. I had a terrible accident, and nobody could help me."

Stories and Poems. Read the children a story. Have them recreate the sequences in pictures.

Read several short poems that contain strong images and have the children illustrate them. A good collection for primary children is *Poems Children Will Sit Still For* by Beatrice Schenk De Regniers, which also includes good suggestions for involving children in the poems.

These activities can be used with limericks and nonsense verses too.

FIGURE 2-2   After reading stories, children enjoy illustrating main ideas of the stories in art activities.

Poetry Club. Create an interest center with poetry books and a small box. Hang a small bulletin board with the following notice on it, and place poetry book jackets around the notice:

POETRY CLUB
1. Find a poem you like.
2. Learn the poem.
3. Write your name, the name of the poem, and the name of the author on a piece of paper and put it in the box.
4. Be on call at all times to recite.

At various times during the day, reach in and draw out a slip of paper. Read the child's name and the poem title. The child recites the poem from memory. (This is a good activity after a test or written work.)

I Don't Like "Don't"—I Don't, I Don't. Use this poem to introduce the activity. Then have the children write or draw the things they don't like.

I hear a million *don'ts* a day.
No matter what I do they say...
   "Now don't do this,
   And don't do that,
   Don't interrupt,
   Don't tease the cat,
   Don't bite your nails,
   Don't slam the door,

Don't leave those messes on the floor.
Don't shout,
Don't fight,
Don't spill your food.
Now don't talk back
And don't be rude."
I don't like *don't* one little bit.
Look! Now they've got me saying it!
         —Lucia and James L. Hymes, Jr.

Story Box. Place a small box in your language arts center. On the outside of the box write, "Put in a thumb and pull out a plum." Inside the box have "starter-uppers" for stories. For example:

- If I were the president I would . . .
- A rose smells sweet because . . .

Also have the first two lines of poems for the children to finish. Keep pencils and paper near the box. Provide a place to sit and write and a place to put the completed work.

Fun Box. Label a large cardboard box in interesting letters "Fun Box." Inside the box put stories, games, puzzles, and comics which have been cut from children's magazines. These may be mounted on colorful construction paper. Sources for material: *Highlights, Jack and Jill, Humpty Dumpty, Children's Digest, Wee Wisdom.* This is good to do after a test or written work.

Sound Families. The children can create fanciful figures using sound families, such as, "an ump lump," "an ock rock," or "an am lamb." They can compose poems or stories using these family sounds and illustrate them.

Play a rhyming game with the children. The teacher gives a word. The children have to think of one word to go with the word given. For the next word given, they have to think of two rhyming words. Continue in this way increasing the number of rhyming words needed.

Fill In the Blanks. Have children write a set of sentences leaving out one word in each. Then they exchange papers and try to fill in the appropriate words.

Have each child bring to the group one sentence encountered in her reading in which she did not recognize a word but figured it out from context. The children share the sentences and discuss the clues used to recognize the word.

In one box place strips with action verbs. In another, place strips with incomplete sentences. The children take turns drawing strips from each box and placing appropriate verbs in sentences. Children who complete the most sentences win. (The missing words can be adjectives, adverbs, or nouns.)

Hilarious stories result when substitutions are made in key parts of a skeleton story.

She is a _____ girl.
She has _____ eyes and _____ hair.
She is very _____.
She likes _____ _____ and _____.
One day a _____ thing happened.
She _____ _____ _____ _____ _____.
(finish story)

Journal of Events. In the science center, set up an interesting experiment, pet, or display. Children observe it daily and keep a journal of their observations. They may wish to draw a picture of what they see each day, too. A personal journal may also be kept about events in their daily lives.

JOURNAL OF EVENTS
Observation

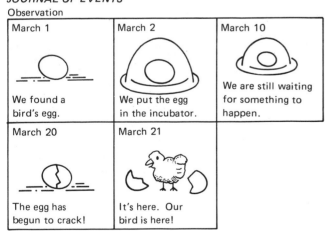

March 1	March 2	March 10
We found a bird's egg.	We put the egg in the incubator.	We are still waiting for something to happen.
March 20	March 21	
The egg has begun to crack!	It's here. Our bird is here!	

Personal

Monday	Tuesday
Plans: I'm spending the night with Nancy.	Plans: I'm going to tell about volcanoes.
Events: Dr. Rights showed the class his Indian relics.	Events: We played kickball. It was fun.

Sentence Sequences. Select a familiar story such as Cinderella. Write sentences about the story on tagboard using main ideas. Let children arrange the strips in sequences.

Have the children write a sequence of three or more steps necessary to each of the following activities:

- Washing the dishes.
- Getting ready for school.
- Washing the car.
- Cleaning a yard.
- Making a sandwich.
- Buying ice cream.
- Mailing a letter.
- Painting a doghouse.

Using Imagination. The teacher starts a story with beginnings such as these: If I were president . . ., If I were a pink kitten . . ., If I could go to the moon . . ., If I had three wishes . . . . Let the children choose the one they like best and write about it. These titles give the children a chance to use their imagination and create. Remind them that in their imagination anything can happen. Have the children write a paper remembering to use all they have learned. Other interesting titles or beginning sentences are:

- And To Think It Happened to Me!
- You Wouldn't Believe It!
- And This Is How It Happened!
- If I Had a Money Tree!

Pictures. Colorful action pictures of children, pets, and storybook characters, mounted on a bulletin board, provide fine inspiration for young writers. A question written below the picture, "Can you write a story about me?" always receives an affirmative answer. Second grade pupils are always eager to select their favorite picture, give the characters names, describe their apparel, and launch forth into a tale of adventure.

Write unfinished sentences on tagboard strips or ditto sheets. Children cut pictures from magazines to complete the sentences, looking for something beginning with the last letter they see. For example: I saw a big o_____. (orange, owl, organ, etc.)

Dictionary Stories. Put letters of the alphabet on tagboard strips. Let children use them to write stories.

These could be called "dictionary stories." Encourage children to use the same letter as much as possible. For example: M—My mother is good. My mother helps me. She helps my brother, too.

Making Sentences Grow. Supply several incomplete sentences for the children to write as many different endings as they can. For example: The mouse ran _____. (into father's shoe, up the clock, into the kitchen)

Spelling.

Toy Box. Select toys or small articles, the names of which have been introduced in spelling, and place them in a small cardboard box. Tape a written list of the contents to the bottom of the box. For example, the box might contain:

- Three-letter words—car, gun, jet, cap, fan, top, dog, hat.
- Blend words—flag, clock, brush, shoe, drum, wheel, spoon.
- Words containing "ar—or"—fork, jar, corn, yarn, scarf, barn, car, cork.

Introduction: "I have put some toys in this box. The names of the toys are words we have been studying in our spelling class. If you would like to practice these words in your free time, you may take the box to your desk. Take out one toy at a time, and try to write its name. When the box is empty, turn it upside down. A list of the toys is written on the bottom of the box. You may check your spelling from this list."

Spelling Word Collections. It is recommended that children develop their own spelling booklets or word lists. These lists can be kept throughout the year and serve as a reference for the child. The word lists may be in the form of an individual word box containing words for the child's booklet or in the form of a master list on which words are clearly marked as mastered or still in need of mastery. Other words in the box are for an expanded list. In the expanded list, the child enters words she thinks she might like to use in writing, words derived from ones she has mastered, and words for which she has looked up synonyms or syllabication or other information in dictionaries.

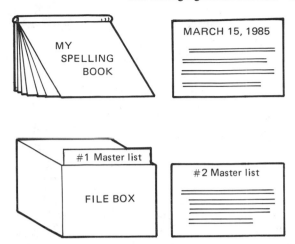

The box should contain 26 stiff guide cards, each with a letter of the alphabet at the top. When a child meets a word she wishes to master or to keep as a reference, she can write it on a piece of paper and file it alphabetically. These cards, possibly illustrated by the child, could also contain meaningful sentences to show correct use of the word.

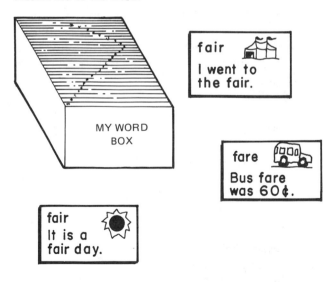

Each week the teacher and child should agree on a group of "spelling words." This will include words that have been misspelled in written work (should be in their word box) and other words usually selected from a basal speller, Dolch Basic Word List, or social studies, science, and math activities. The number of words on each list will vary according to the skill of the child.

Definitions. This is a game for two teams. Team A reads its definitions aloud and Team B tries to recognize the words being defined. One point is scored for each correct response. Team B then reads to Team A.

Spelling Teamwork. Designate two chairs with back covers or labels as "team study chairs." Provide a small blackboard, if you like. Two children use their group spelling word box or individual word boxes and practice spelling and writing words together.

RECEPTIVE LANGUAGE

Listening

Sequence

- Describe a scene (perhaps from a story that is about to be read) item by item. For example: "There is a big farm house. Behind the farm house is a big tree. In the tree is a bird's nest." Have the children draw each item and put it in the proper location as you describe it. At the end, each picture will probably be quite different.
- Make several sounds such as snapping fingers, tapping toe, and humming. Have the child listen with her eyes closed, then imitate the sounds she heard.
- Read sentences such as these, and have the children tell the rhyming words they hear:

    It is *fun* to *run* in the *sun.*
    Ten men made the rabbit *pen.*
    Mother will *make* and *bake* a *cake.*
    Mother will *let* you *get* the *pet.*
    Jack can carry the *sack* on his *back.*

- Read the following poem or a nursery rhyme and have the child repeat the rhyming words. Or read the poem leaving out the last word of every other line and have the child fill in the missing rhyming words.

    ### Indian Children
    Where we walk to school each day
    Indian children used to play—
    All about our native land,
    Where the shops and houses stand.
    —Annette Wynne

Oral Directions

- Tell students you are going to make several mistakes on purpose during the day and at the end of the day you will ask them to tell you what they were. For example: misspell a word, mispronounce a word, call a student by the wrong name.
- This game works best with small groups. Give several directions for one person on each team to follow. The one that follows the directions exactly wins a point. For example: Go to the pencil sharpener, turn around three times, skip to the window, and then jump up.
- "Do As I Say" is a game in which the class listens carefully to a set of directions and then tries to follow them exactly. Try these types of directions (say them all while everyone listens—no writing or questions):

    Write your name on the last line of your paper.
    Write the numbers from 1 to 10 all on line four.
    Write the colors of our flag on line ten.
    (Repeat the directions twice; then students act.)

    All boys with blue eyes are to line up against the back wall.
    All girls with brown eyes stand near the windows.
    Boys with brown eyes line up near the door.
    Girls with blue eyes stand in front of the chalkboard.

20 Questions. This game can be played by individuals or by a large group. Children ask questions that can be answered only by "yes" or "no." The object is to guess the title of a book a child has read. Children quickly learn to ask categorical questions such as: Is it fiction? Does it take place in modern times? Is it about a real or imaginary animal? The questioning continues until all 20 questions are asked or the title is guessed.

Three Directions at Once. For this activity you will need a variety of colored chalk and a list of words. Direct a child to do these three things:

1. Find a word or word part.
2. Use a particular color of chalk.
3. Draw a circle, box, line, etc., around, under, or above the word. Example: Teacher says, "Mary, find a word that has a short *a* in the list and put two lines under it with green chalk."

Reading.

Book Party. Let the students plan a book party where each one will portray a favorite character from a book. Each student can make simple costumes using paper, unbleached muslin, or old clothes that can be decorated appropriately with crayon. Have each child enact an interesting part of the book. Several children may represent characters from the same book with all sharing in the same short presentation.

Book Worm. As a child completes a book, let her add a segment to the body of a long Book Worm, which can encircle the room on the wall above the boards and windows. The child prints the title and author of the book she has read on a piece of bright construction paper, which is trimmed to resemble part of the body. The body continues to grow behind the head which one student has designed.

Book Jacket Puzzles. To help encourage interest in reading, the teacher can mount book jackets on heavy cardboard and cut them into puzzles. A frame can be made by cutting the center out of one piece of corrugated cardboard and gluing the border to a second piece the same size. The outlines of the puzzle pieces can be marked on the frame as a guide for the children to follow. The books are handy for reading when the puzzles are completed.

Word Recognition. Ask the following questions and riddles.

- It is something used to hit a ball. It rhymes with *cat* and *hat*.
- It is something you drink. It rhymes with *bee* and *tree*.
- You might do this to your shoe. It rhymes with *fly* and *pie*.

FIGURE 2–3 Interest whale: Each of the stars on the whale indicates a book read by the child.

- It is a number. It rhymes with *blue* and *shoe*.
- What does a dog have that rhymes with *nail*?
- What color rhymes with *shoe*?
- What are you wearing that rhymes with *blocks*?
- What is a married woman called that rhymes with *knife*?

Rhyming Words. For this rhyming activity a shoe box with a picture of a dog is used. Cut a hole in the dog's mouth so that tongue depressors can be inserted. On each side of the tongue depressor or "bone" write rhyming words. As the child says the words on both sides of the "bone," she can feed the dog the bone.

Families on Rhyming Street. Draw large houses on construction paper. To each house attach a list of rhyming words. These houses and their families may be placed on a bulletin board in a street scene. Mail boxes may be labeled with the "family" name. Example: all, at, ill.

Five Senses (Independent or group activity). Use cards labeled with the words "smell," "see," "touch," "taste," and "hear." Place a group of pictures with these words. Let children group the pictures with an appropriate card.

Name the Children. Place many pictures of children on sheets of paper. Let children give them names. Create dialogue for make-believe situations. For example: a trip to the zoo. This activity can also be done with pictures of animals.

Treasure Chest. Place pictures in a box which has been decorated to resemble a treasure chest. Place along the chalkboard ledge words that describe the pictures in the box. Choose a child to pick a "treasure" and then find the word card that describes the picture.

Rebus. Write a story on a 9″ X 12″ sheet of tagboard. Omit some words that are in the children's reading vocabulary. Draw a picture "clue" for each omitted word. Under each picture cut a small triangular slot. Make 1″ X 2″ cards showing the missing words. Put these cards in an envelope and clip the envelope to the tagboard story sheet. The children are to take the word cards out of the envelope and lay them face up on their desks. Next, they are to start reading the story. Each time they come to a missing word, they are to find the card which says that word and place it in the appropriate slot.

Look and Find. Show and discuss a particularly difficult word card. Then place it in the pack. Expose the cards rapidly. The watching children quietly clap their hands when the hidden card is exposed.

Stop and Go. Prepare several red and green cards and place them in the pack of word cards to be reviewed. Allow one child to say the words on the cards as they are exposed until she meets a red, or Stop, card. Then another child will take her place. If a child meets a green, or Go, card, she may continue.

Word Hospital. Children help cure patients by learning new words. Make a "word hospital" on tagboard, ditto, or flannel board, depending on how you want to use this activity. Make beds using felt markers. Make words movable by putting them on slips of paper or labeling tape (the kind that will restick). As a word is learned, it is moved from a bed to a section for cured patients.

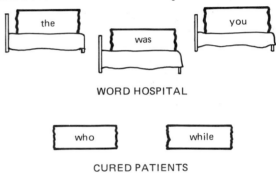

Bean Bag Game. Make up the board on a piece of heavy 36″ X 45″ paper. The child throws a bean bag, hitting

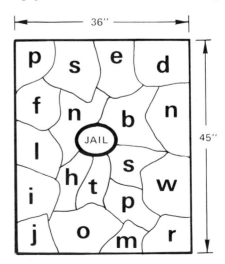

one of the letters and gives a word which begins with the sound of the letter hit. If she lands in jail she stays until she can help someone who misses.

Wheel of Chance. A large cardboard clockface is numbered from 1 to 12 and fitted with a large movable hand. The hand can be held in place by means of a large fastener. Alongside the clockface 12 words or phrases are printed either on the blackboard or on a large sheet of paper. A child is called on; she flicks the hand, sees the number at which it stops, then reads the corresponding printed word or phrase.

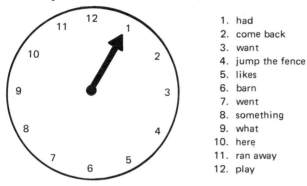

1. had
2. come back
3. want
4. jump the fence
5. likes
6. barn
7. went
8. something
9. what
10. here
11. ran away
12. play

Pick a Slip. Write single words or phrases on slips of heavy paper. Write a number from 1 to 3 in the upper right-hand corner of each slip. Two or more players may play. Slips are placed face down on the table.

A GARDEN OF WORDS . . .

FIGURE 2–4 Flower centers turn to make words.

Players take turns selecting a slip and reading it. If the player reads it correctly, she keeps the slip. If not, she replaces it on the table. Add the numbers on each player's slips and the highest score wins.

A Race to the Moon. Divide the group into three teams. A member of each team is called upon in turn to pick out from the words you have displayed or written on the board the one you say aloud. The team member must go up, underline, and carefully repeat the word you say. When a correct answer is given, the space ship moves a step nearer the moon (erase one of the lines en route to the moon). First team to reach the moon is the winner.

First Team Over. Draw chalk lines on the floor to show starting and finishing lines. Line children up behind the starting lines in two teams. The teacher or group leader shows a word card. The two children who are first in line compete to say the word correctly and the first one to do so moves to the finish line. Another word is shown. The first team with all its players behind the finish line wins.

Wordo. On ditto sheets make word Bingo cards that can be used by a class or a group of children. These different sheets may be made with the same words but arranged in different order. Give every third child the same sheet. The teacher calls out a word (writing it on the board if she wishes) and the child covers it on her card. At some point in the game the teacher makes sure that one sheet has a row covered so someone will call "Wordo." At that point, every child in the third position should call it too.

Beginning Sounds.
Beginning Sounds Hunt. Walk through the house or stroll through the dime store collecting small bottles, lace, a watch, figurines, models, utensils, anything that can be kept in a box. Let pupils sort materials of this type into small trays or boxes labeled with the beginning

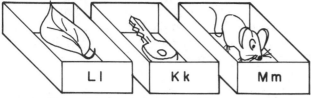

sound of the object. A teacher might concentrate on just a few consonants, a few vowels, or the entire alphabet.

Surprise Box. Place in a box small objects such as miniature toys, a button, ruler, pencil, shell, marble, bead, spool, scissors, etc. The child reaches into the box and pulls out an object. She names the object and then gives another word that begins with the same sound. Continue until all the objects are out. Change the objects in the box from time to time.

Boat Race. Put the following illustration on the blackboard and divide the group into two teams. Have a boat race between the two teams to see which team's boat can reach the dock first. Each time a member of a team answers a question correctly (for example: Name an object whose name begins with d) a square is checked. If the answer is wrong, the question goes to the other team. The team whose squares are checked off first is the winner.

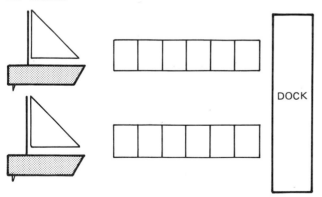

The Bus Ride. Start with this question, "What would you take on a bus ride whose name begins with a __?" The child must then name an object whose name begins with the designated letter.

Or start with this phrase, "I went to the supermarket to buy something that begins with __," and have class members name articles with the same beginning sound.

Merry-Go-Round. Cut out a circle about 10″ in diameter from tagboard. Cut out another circle about an inch smaller. Attach the two wheels by means of a brass brad in the center. Draw a red arrow on the large circle pointing toward the smaller one. Print consonants at evenly spaced intervals close to the edge of the smaller circle. Spin and take a ride by giving a word beginning with the sound of the letter on which the arrow lands.

Build a House. Make a large, simple outline of a house on the board. Ask the children to help put the "bricks" on the house, adding a brick every time another rhyming word is given.

Baseball Game. This can be adapted for initial consonants, ending sounds, blends, rhyming words, and long or short vowels. A baseball diamond is made on tagboard or on the board, or you may use the corners of the room for the bases. Each player tries to make a home run by thinking of a word that begins with the letter on each base. Change the letters as desired. You may divide the group into teams and keep score of home runs.

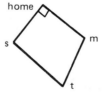

How Does Your Garden Grow? Pass out large pieces of drawing paper that have examples of word parts written on small circles and the title "How Does Your Garden Grow?" is written at the top. The children are to make flowers by placing petals around the circle centers. On each petal, they write a word formed by placing a blend or a consonant before the word part on the center.

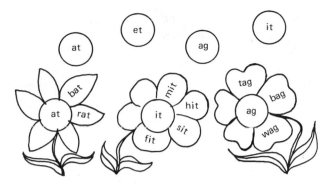

Word Wheel. Cut out a circle about 6″ in diameter from tagboard. Cut out another circle about an inch smaller. Attach the two by means of a brass fastener in the center. Select words beginning with the consonant or blend the pupils need to practice. Print the endings at evenly spaced intervals close to the edge of the larger circle. Print the consonant or blend close to the edge of the smaller circle. When the wheel is turned, entire words can be seen. Children take turns pronouncing them.

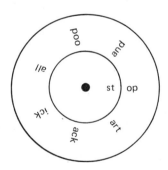

Hopscotch. Draw a hopscotch court on a large piece of tagboard. Pupils may use buttons to mark their places. When the pupil hops into a square, she must say a word beginning with the blend in that square or start over at her next turn.

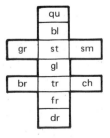

Railroad Conductor. Draw a train on the blackboard. Write consonant blends above the smokestack instead of smoke. Say, "Have you ever seen a talking train? Here is one that can talk. It is telling us the names of the stations where it will stop. You may be the conductor on this train and call out the stations where it will stop." One child at a time can call the names, or the class can call them together.

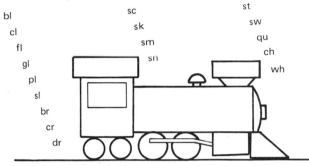

My Book of Sounds. Staple 26 blank pages together to form a booklet. Print an alphabet letter, capital and lowercase, on each page. Using old magazines or catalogs, let the children find and paste pictures on each page of objects whose names begin with that letter. Variation: Endings to words may also be placed one to a sheet. Child then may make sentences using words having that ending, as shown in the example.

Alphabet Bingo. On tagboard or cardboard, rule off squares and print different letters of the alphabet. The child picks up picture cards or toys and identifies their beginning (or ending) sounds. She places a marker on her bingo card if she has the matching sound.

Alphabet Game. Letter cards of all 26 letters will be needed for each two children. Put each set into a manila envelope. Give one envelope to each pair of children playing the game. Place cards face down between the two opponents. Each one draws a card in turn. If the player draws a vowel, she places it, face up, in one pile before her. Consonants are placed in another pile. *W* or *Y* are not placed in either pile but put aside. *W* and *Y* each count two points; *a, e, i, o,* and *u* each count one point. The winner is the one who gets the most points.

Consonant and Vowel Sounds. In teaching letter sounds it may be helpful to identify as many of them as possible with familiar sounds. For example:

- *wh* What sound do you make when you blow out candles?
- *r* What sound does the lion make?
- *sh* What sound means "Be quiet"?
- *ch* What sound do you make when you sneeze?
- *ow* What sound do you make when you hurt yourself? (au)
- *ow* What sound do you make when you are surprised? (oh!)
- *oo* What sound does the wind make when it blows around the house?
- *s* What sound does the radiator make when steam is coming out?
- *gr* What sound does a dog make when she growls?
- *m* What sound do you make when you eat something very good?

Bingo Song. The children will enjoy learning vowels by singing these verses to the familiar tune of "Bingo."

There are some vowels we all know,
And this is how they sound—
Ă Ĕ Ĭ Ŏ Ŭ
Ă Ĕ Ĭ Ŏ Ŭ
Ă Ĕ Ĭ Ŏ Ŭ
Are our short vowel sounds.

There are some vowels we all know,
And this is how they sound—
Ā Ē Ī Ō Ū
Ā Ē Ī Ō Ū
Ā Ē Ī Ō Ū
Are our long vowel sounds.

Note: The children may like to leave out one sound and clap, then snap their fingers. This may be done with spelling words also.

Tic Tac Toe. Draw a tic tac toe diagram and place a word in the center that has the vowel sound you want children to use in their words. Players write a word in any square using that same vowel sound. The first student to get words in a row wins. If neither wins, Ms. Vowel gets the point. *Note:* Children should initial their words.

Parade of the Vowels. Draw a parade of long vowels on the blackboard. Give each vowel stick legs. Say, "Can you name the vowels in this parade? First tell me the vowel's name, and then tell me the sound that vowel makes when it is long, or give a word containing that long vowel sound. Variation: Using the same idea, have a parade of short vowels.

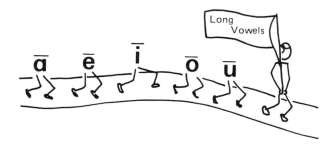

Magical E *Game.* Make word cards of words with short vowels that make new words when an *e* is added. Make a card with an *e* on it. Word cards might be: pin, cap, at, fat, hat, mat, nap. Children take turns pronouncing words with short vowels and then adding the "magical *e*" and pronouncing the new words that are formed.

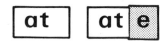

SUMMARY

This unit has encouraged you to experiment with many activities to make the language arts program interesting and meaningful for young children. The unit contains a variety of activities to develop the expressive and receptive language arts skills: speaking, listening, reading, and writing (both composing and forming letters or "handwriting"). You are encouraged to experiment in the classroom to find out which activities best suit the needs of the children in your group. Because of the wide range of abilities present in any early elementary grade, no specific grade level has been assigned to these activities. You should feel free to adapt them to the interests, needs, and abilities of each child. Your knowledge of the child will be the ultimate basis for any grade designation.

LEARNING ACTIVITIES

A. Using an opaque projector, project a favorite cartoon character onto a large sheet of paper taped onto a wall. Trace the character. Use magic markers to color in the figure. If possible, laminate the finished product. Use the character to stimulate a composing activity with a group of children. For example: This is Donald Duck. He just had a big surprise; tell about it (or write about it).

B. Start a card file of sentences to use for composing "starters." Organize the cards according to topic and grade level.

C. Use an overhead projector in a handwriting lesson. Have individual children come up and write their letters on the transparency for all to see their prowess with handwriting.

D. Use one of the reading games in the unit with a small group of children. Evaluate your experience. Share your results with the class. What would you change or keep the same in the activity? Why?

E. Obtain a school supply catalog. Choose three items you would purchase for your language arts center. Explain why you would purchase them, including the price and the specific skill it would be used for.

F. Choose one of the poems from Unit 1. Read it to a group of children to reinforce listening skills. Prepare some open-ended questions on the poem to encourage close listening. Evaluate your experience. Share your results with the class.

G. Go through the newspaper. Pick out an especially large and attractive advertisement for a bicycle, toy, or anything else of high interest to children. Bring the advertisement to the classroom and have the children suggest wording for it. They may want to draw up their own version of the ad.

UNIT REVIEW

1. List at least three activities that you would use to teach listening skills. Explain your choices.
2. Describe at least three activities you would use to help children develop speaking skills. Explain your choices.
3. List at least three activities for writing (forming letters) and three for composing. Give your rationale for these choices.
4. Choose at least three reading activities you would use with children in the early elementary grades. Give the reasons for your choices.

ADDITIONAL READING

Composing Skills

Barbe, Walter B. *Creative Writing Activities Handbook, Highlights Fun-Do-Packs.* Columbus, Ohio: Highlights for Children, 1975. Elementary prose and poetry ideas suitable for grades 2–6.

Creative Teaching Press. *Recipes for Creative Writing.* New York: Creative Teaching Press, 1977. Available on primary or intermediate level, a "recipe box" of plot ideas, visual stimuli, and story starters.

DeRegniers, Beatrice Schenk. *Poems Children Will Sit Still For.* New York: Citation Press, 1969.

The Education Center. *Kids' Cards Creative Writing.* Greensboro, N.C.: The Education Center, 1977. Packs of 96 cards available on primary (1–4) or intermediate (3–6) levels. Very good writing stimuli.

Forte, Imogene, et al. *Cornering Creative Writing: Kids' Stuff Basic Series.* Buffalo, N.Y.: Incentive Publications, 1976. A wonderful collection of free choice activities for teaching creative writing, including use of learning centers (K–6).

Hymes, James L., Jr., and Hymes, Lucia. *Hooray for Chocolate.* Columbus, Ohio: Chas. E. Merrill, 1981.

Tovey, Duane R. *Writing Centers in the Elementary School.* Bloomington, Ind.: Phi Delta Kappa Educational Foundation, 1979. Outlines ways to collect activities and materials for use in setting up writing centers in the elementary classroom.

Zavatsky, Bill, and Padgett, Ron. (eds.) *The Whole Word Catalogue, 2.* New York: McGraw-Hill, 1977. Gives lots of ideas ranging from gimmicks to involvement with art, video, television, ecology, and history. Includes how-to's of poetry and prose.

Language Arts Resources

Karnes, Marle B. *Helping Young Children Develop Language Skills.* Arlington, Va.: The Council for Exceptional Children, 1976.

Schubert, Delwyn A. (ed.) *Reading Games That Teach.* Monterey Park, Calif.: Creative Teaching Press, 1965.

Unit 3 Special Topics in Language Arts

OBJECTIVES

After studying this unit, you will be able to

- describe at least two positive teaching techniques using television in the early elementary language arts program.
- list six guidelines for using television with young children.
- discuss four effects of television on children's behavior, based on research findings.
- list seven suggestions for providing nonsexist language arts experiences in the early elementary grades.

In this unit two aspects of the language arts program for the early elementary grades are discussed. These are (1) the place of television and (2) nonsexist language arts experiences.

TELEVISION AND LANGUAGE ARTS

Just as you must work *with* each child's developmental interest level in all language arts activities, the teacher in the following example realized quickly that she had to work *with*—not against—television in her classroom. Reading this teacher's story should demonstrate how to make TV a positive language arts experience for a first grade class.

Teaching Report: Using TV to Teach Thinking Skills

In the fall, 28 squiggly first grade boys and one girl swarmed into my classroom. With that group of children—most of them immature, most of them repeaters—I used traditional elementary teacher's tools and failed immediately. For two incredibly long days, I found nothing that could hold the attention of these youngsters for longer than a minute. Then I discovered their interest in TV and started a brand new career—TV educator.

I discovered the children liked to dictate stories that centered exclusively on *Batman,* at that time a TV program that ranked as a before-school favorite. They knew all the details of the show. They talked about it with intense interest and acted out parts. While they dictated, I wrote down what they said. Then had them read their stories back to me.

As they recounted the adventures of Batman, I was able to sneak in some real lessons. I introduced the skill of prediction: What do you think will happen next? Then I discussed sequence: What did Robin do next? Then, comparison: How is this show like *Gilligan's Island?*

One television-related activity led to another. Eventually, the students were willing to chart stories that were not all television-related, while retaining their super interest in their superhero. They also were able to answer rather difficult questions about other TV shows. In fact, they answered questions far beyond what one would normally expect of first graders—much less underachievers. They learned to think, and they had a good time.

Whenever the subject was television programs—plots, stars, or characters—the children were the experts. I used familiar material as the subject for hard questions—questions that would teach children to think, analyze, and extrapolate. Previously, I had been mistaken to ask children hard questions about unfamiliar material. No one, after all, would dare ask me a higher-order question about astrophysics.

These television-related questioning techniques in this class led me to understand the positive use of TV in promoting thinking skills. (Potter, 1982)

It's clear from the report that many of the same positive teaching techniques with television would fit nicely into the primary language arts program. It certainly is a more practical approach to work *with* television and young children when you consider recent statistics which show that young children (under age nine) watch TV on the average of four hours per day. (U.S. Bureau of the Census, 1981). Some additional suggestions on how to use television with young children follow.

Guidelines for TV and Young Children. Television viewing is rapidly becoming the favorite passtime of children. This can be good and it can be bad. It is hoped that the following suggestions will be helpful in guiding young children's TV experiences.

- Use TV schedules from magazines or newspapers to discuss with children the programs they watch. Help them learn to select the best ones available.

  Read the schedule with the children. Ask them which programs they plan to watch. Talk about why one program might be a better choice than another. It may be the viewing hours. It may be what the show is about. Tell children what *you* think about certain programs.

  Use TV guides as a reading resource in your language arts center to spark interest.

- Many programs encourage the viewer's participation by directing the viewer to perform specific activities. These programs are good for young children. It is better for a young child to be an *active* viewer than a passive one.

- Encourage children not to sit too close to the TV set. TV can be bad for the pupils of the eyes if watched too closely.

- Encourage the children to change positions or angles as they watch TV. Be sure to stress good posture.

- Encourage frequent TV "breaks." It is helpful for children not only to *move* around, but also to *look* around.

- Don't use the TV set as a "babysitter" in the classroom by turning it on and then attending to classroom chores. TV should be a "learning machine" as well as an "enjoyment machine."

- *Participate* in viewing with the children. Use the TV to develop language, perceptual, and other developmental skills: "Do you see that?" "Look at that!" "What did he say?" "What did that word mean?" "Why do you think that was so funny?" "Remember when we saw an elephant like that?"

- Many programs are designed for young children. Plan to watch them with the children in your class. Plan activities around these programs when possible.

- Relate objects and events to what is seen on TV. "See that dog? It looks just like the one we see on TV. What is his name?"

- Don't let yourself or the children become addicted to television.

Try planning language arts activities like the following one to use TV in a positive way.

Sample Activity: Using TV in Language Arts
1. Make a simple TV Plan like the one illustrated.
2. Read the TV schedule to the children or let them read it. Ask them to write down their choices on a TV plan. If they can't write yet, have them tell you how to fill in the chart.
3. Post the chart in a special place near the TV set. Put a pencil on a string by it.
4. For at least three days, fill in the charts with the programs watched by the children.
5. Be on the lookout for too much TV watching!

TV PLAN			
Date	Time	Program Name	Channel

Working with young children means working with youngsters who spend a good deal of time watching TV outside the classroom. Use the guidelines as a starting point for working with TV in a positive way in early childhood language arts.

EFFECTS OF WATCHING TELEVISION ON CHILDREN'S BEHAVIOR

Much attention is given to television commercials and their effects on children, but what are some of the other effects of television viewing in general? A review of recent research (Cater and Strickland, 1977; Comstock, et al., 1978; Cook, et al., 1975; Stein and Friedrich, 1971) indicates the following:

- Television program content can have a negative effect on children's behavior, and that effect is likely to be a long-term one. More superficially, watching aggressive and violent programs tends to increase aggressive behavior in young children.
- What children bring to the viewing experience (states of arousal, anger, excitement, and so forth) can modify the effect that a given program has on their behavior.
- Programs showing prosocial (helping, sharing, cooperative) behavior can increase such behavior in young children.
- Educational content—as in "Sesame Street," for example—can facilitate children's concepts and vocabulary development.

Thus, children can learn from television. There is no moratorium on learning when they sit in front of the television set. While there is still much that is not known about television and its effects, we do know that it is a real part of the child's daily learning experience.

Effects of Television Commercials on Children. The average child between the ages of two and eleven is exposed to more than 20,000 commercials a year. Many of these commercials are designed especially for young children, and it seems that their techniques succeed; children are affected by television advertising. They draw conclusions about things (if it's on television, it must be good), they prefer advertised over non-advertised products, and they implore their parents to buy advertised goods (Adler, 1977). There are side effects. Children develop materialistic values (Goldberg, Gorn, and Givson, 1978). Commercials carry an underlying message—to consume is to be happy (Roberts et al., 1978).

The food commercials that young children see usually display highly sugared foods (cereals, candy bars, fruit-flavored drinks). As many as two-thirds of commercials associated with children's television programs are for such sugared snacks (Barcus, 1975a). The simple fact that these commercials are repeated so frequently during the hours of children's programming time may also increase the attractiveness of these advertised foods, thereby affecting food preferences.

Young children need to be educated about food—what it is for, how it is related to their health and well-being, how it is produced and consumed. Part of educating for responsible citizenship means recognizing waste and irresponsible consumption. According to Joan Gussow (1977):

Food ads on television surely fail to teach children that food comes not from plants in Battle Creek, but from plants that require clean air, clean water, and fertile topsoil to sustain them. Certainly blue, pink, orange, and yellow confections—urged upon children as essential components of a good breakfast—must confuse children about the reality of food: its sources, its nature, its role in human life.

Children are little consumers, exercising their preferences through their parents' wallets and shopping habits. Parents usually yield to the persuasion of their young children in the selection of breakfast cereals and snack foods. In a study of families with five- to seven-year-old children, almost 90 percent of the parents reported that they usually accepted their children's preferences in cereals, and more than half reported that they usually yielded to their children's choice of snack foods (Ward and Wackman, 1977). Joan Gussow sums it up nicely:

It is probably not necessary to point out that the increasing emphasis on "nutrition" in food advertising seldom has anything to do with the products' real nutritional value to the folks who will be consuming them. In the United States and in Canada, vitamin and mineral deficiencies—at least deficiencies of what advertisers bill as the "important" vitamins and minerals—would appear to represent a very minor proportion of nutrition-related disorders.... On the other hand, degenerative diseases associated with over consumption—of calories, of saturated fats, of refined carbohydrates, and possibly of animal protein as well—are becoming epidemic. The addition of vitamins and minerals to products which are low in fiber and high in salt, sugar, saturated fat, modified starches, and other fillers does not make them nutritious (though nutrient information carried on their labels may, unfortunately, help convince children—and their parents—that they are). (Gussow, 1977)

NONSEXIST LANGUAGE ARTS

A major social development of young children in the early elementary grades is the acquisition of a sex role identity. Very simply, they learn through real-life experiences as well as through school books and other materials what it means to be a girl or a boy.

Since it is important that youngsters have the opportunity to grow and develop to their maximum potential, it is important that the books and other language arts materials used should not limit that potential but rather fit developmental levels, which are the same for both sexes. Figure 3–1 defines some basic terms used in the following discussion.

Anyone who works with young children must be aware of the great influence they have on children whenever they have different standards for males and females and, thus, treat them differently. Even more important in language arts, the books and materials used can give young children very clear messages about what are considered the "right" behavior, traits, and values for persons of their sex. Let us consider some ways to choose books and materials for young children that show boys and girls (and men and women, too) in an equal, unbiased way.

Checklist for Providing Nonsexist Experiences.

- Look for books and materials with nonstereotyped images of boys and girls, men and women. (Are all women "nurses or mommies"; all men "rough and tough"?)
- Check books and materials for sexist language. (Examples: "sissy," "little lady," "real little man," "Boys don't cry.")
- Use nonsexist books and other materials in language arts activities and centers. (Example: *Free to Be– You and Me* by Thomas, Steinem, and Pogrebin. See end of unit for further suggestions.)
- Initiate and guide activities designed to provide all students with the chance to develop all types of skills. (Examples: both girls and boys at woodworking bench, in the housekeeping corner, with the large wheel toys.)
- Use nonsexist language with the children. Consider the following examples and the different messages they send to young children:
  - "Mike, I'm really proud of how you played on the bars today. Lisa, you look lovely today. Is that a new dress you're wearing?"
  - "Donna and Peter, you're late for school again. (Harsh tones) Peter, I am absolutely not going to put up with this tardy behavior any longer. It's a half hour after school for you, young man. You sit down and get right to work. And Donna (voice softens), a nice young lady like you—you should know better than this. Now I don't expect to see any more of this behavior from you."
- Use pictures on classroom walls which depict men, women, boys, and girls in nonstereotypical roles.
- Plan for and encourage boys and girls to play together in as many situations as possible. Do not always leave this up to the children in the free play period.
- Assign classroom jobs to both girls and boys. Don't make special jobs just for boys or just for girls.

Sex Bias or Sex Role Stereotyping: The unconscious and conscious values and assumptions which stereotype the sexes and channel females and males toward those interests, activities, and goals considered "appropriate" for their sex.

Sex Discrimination: Limiting a person's opporrunities, rewards, or status on the basis of sex; usually thought of as practices which can be proved, particularly in a court of law.

Sexism: Attitudes and actions which relegate women to a secondary and inferior status.

Sexist Content: (1) Presents more male than female characters; (2) portrays males in a wider variety of occupations than females; (3) shows a majority of female characters in passive, subordinate, and incompetent roles, and a majority of male characters in active, dominant, and capable roles; (4) assigns desirable personality traits to males and undesirable ones to females.

Sexist Literature: Reading that not only makes value judgements on the basis of sex but also reinforces stereotypical differences between girls and boys.

FIGURE 3–1 Important terms for early childhood teachers to know

HOW SEXIST ARE YOU? A TEST FOR TEACHERS

Directions: Answer the following questions Yes or No according to the way you behave.
Complete the essay question. Then score yourself as directed.

	YES	NO
1. Do you ask only boys to do heavy work and perform executive duties in the classroom, and only girls to do light work and clean up?	___	___
2. Do you pity girls who are unable or unwilling to be fashionable?	___	___
3. Do you call special attention to girls who *are* fashionable?	___	___
4. Do you pity boys who are unable or unwilling to be athletic?	___	___
5. Do you call special attention to boys who *are* athletic?	___	___
6. Do you react negatively to boys who are not aggressive and to girls who are?	___	___
7. Do you plan different activities or different adaptations of the same activity for boys and for girls, primarily because of sex?	___	___
8. Does the content you use include more exciting role models for boys than for girls? Does this material stereotype women as housewives, mothers, or workers in menial or supportive positions?	___	___
9. Do you ever use such slang terms as "sissy," "tomboy," "chick," or "broad"?	___	___
10. Do you make generalizations like "Boys shouldn't hit girls" or "Ladies don't talk that way" or "Ladies before gentlemen"?	___	___
11. Do you expect girls to be more verbal and artistic than boys, or boys to be more mathematical and scientific than girls?	___	___
12. Do you feel it is more important to help boys sort out career options than to help girls do the same?	___	___
13. Do you tend to discipline girls verbally and leniently and boys physically and strictly?	___	___

Essay Question: They may act exactly the same way, but they are called absentminded
if they are men and scatterbrained if they are women; intellectually curious if they are men
and schemers if they are women; sensitive if they are men and emotional if they are women;
logical if they are men and intuitive if they are women.

Directions: Respond logically or intuitively to the statement you have just read.

HOW TO SCORE YOURSELF: Give yourself 5 points for each No answer, and 30 points for
good logic on the essay question (0 points for intuition). Do not mark on a curve. If your score
is below 90, meet with your classmates and plan your own consciousness-raising group.

FIGURE 3–2 Self-awareness Questionnaire

(Examples: Both boys and girls wash out cups and sweep the floor.)

- Discuss with the children such questions as:

  How many mothers work somewhere else besides at home?

  What kind of jobs do mothers and fathers have?

  What do mothers and fathers do for their own enjoyment?

  What do mothers do for children? What do fathers do for children?

  Would your parents treat you differently if you were a girl/boy? How?

  What toys do you think are for girls? for boys? Have you ever wanted or ever had a toy that is supposed to be *for the other sex?*

  How do you feel about a girl who can run faster than a boy?

  What sports are for girls? for boys?

  Do you think a woman would be a good president of the United States?

  Have you ever seen a man cry? Have you ever seen a woman cry? How did you feel?

- Now, complete the Self-awareness Questionnaire in Figure 3–2 and find out the areas you need to work on to become more nonsexist in your own attitudes.

SUMMARY

TV can be a positive learning experience for young children if it is used with care and made part of language arts experiences. Guidelines for TV and young children include helping them use TV schedules to select their programs, sit a good distance from the TV set, change positions while watching, and take frequent breaks from watching. Research indicates that TV programs and commercials do affect children's behavior. It is up to their teachers, among others, to recognize these effects and counter them. For example, teaching about nutrition is important, because children's TV commercials place heavy emphasis on sugary snacks.

A major social development of children in the early elementary grades is the acquisition of a sex role identity. To avoid sex bias, which can lead to sex discrimination, teachers must have the same standards for both boys and girls. Children's books can also influence their ideas about sex roles, behavior, and many other important areas of life. Neither the teacher's language and attitudes nor the language arts materials should contain sex stereotyped references.

LEARNING ACTIVITIES

A. Watch an hour or two of children's programs on a Saturday morning. During your viewing time, record the following information:

  - Number of commercials.
  - Topics of commercials.
  - How many nutritious foods were advertised.
  - How many "junk" foods were advertised.

  Discuss your record of observations with your classmates. How do your findings match the research findings referred to in this unit?

B. Bring at least six early elementary level children's books to class. Rate each of the books for bias according to the checklist for nonsexist materials provided in this unit. Decide which of your books is the least sexist and which is the most. Remember to include the illustrations in your evaluation. Explain your choices.

C. Role play with a classmate: One is a parent and the other a child watching TV together. You hear a sugary cereal commercial saying, "Ask Mom to make it part of your good breakfast." Have both parent and child give their reasons (valid and nonvalid) for or against the commercial.

D. Choose a TV program that is popular with the children of elementary age that you know. Design some language arts activities around this program. If possible, try out your activities with a group of children. Evaluate your experience and share the results with your classmates.

E. Visit an early elementary grade classroom. Spend an hour observing for sexist and nonsexist materials and practices. Record your findings. Share them with your classmates. Be sure to include your own suggestions on how to improve situations that need improvement.

F. Role play a teacher (1) making sexist comments and (2) making nonsexist comments.

G. In a classroom setting, take a survey of children's favorite TV programs. How many are cartoons? How many are animal shows? How many are adult shows? How many shows (on the average) does each child watch on Saturdays? How many hours of television viewing does this translate into?

ACTIVITIES FOR CHILDREN

A. Have the children write and illustrate TV commercials for one or more of the following:
   1. Favorite food.
   2. New invention.
   3. New toy.
   4. Robot that does homework.
   5. Vacation trip to another planet.
   They may want to read and act out these commercials to the class.

B. Have the children pretend to be TV commentators at a special children's event, such as a junior olympics, an art contest, a circus, or a children's parade. Have the children prepare questions to ask the participants at the event. Use props (desk, name card, microphone) to add a more dramatic touch.

C. Ask the children to make a list of their favorite TV characters (or dictate the list to you). Make a master list and either display it on a chart or write it on the blackboard. Read it aloud and discuss the children's choices with them. Let them give you reasons for their choices.

D. Using the master list of favorite TV characters, play a guessing game, giving clues to the favorite character for others to guess the identity.

E. Have children write a story, poem, or short description of their favorite TV cartoon character or personality. They may draw a picture illustrating their story or poem.

F. Ask the children to write (or dictate) endings to an incomplete story about a popular cartoon character. Then share their stories at story time and give credit to the "authors."

G. Have children make up a story about a favorite TV cartoon character and tape the story. Put the tape in the listening center for other children to enjoy.

H. List on the blackboard several occupations, such as doctor, car mechanic, house painter, teacher, nurse, secretary, and veterinarian. Have the children tell you if (1) men, (2) women, or (3) both men and women can be in each occupation. Discuss the results of this activity with the children, noting any role stereotyping to work on in future lessons.

UNIT REVIEW

1. Why is it necessary to work *with* television in the language arts program?
2. What are some language arts activities that lend themselves to television viewing? Give specific examples.
3. Give six guidelines for young children's TV viewing.
4. List four specific research findings on the effects of TV viewing on children's behavior.
5. List four effects of television commercials on young children, as evidenced in research.
6. What messages about food tend to be sent by commercials on children's TV programs?
7. List seven suggestions for providing nonsexist language arts experiences.
8. Define the terms *sex bias, sex discrimination, sexism, sexist content,* and *sexist literature.*

ADDITIONAL READINGS

The Effects of Television

Adler, R. *Research on the Effects of Television Advertising on Children.* Washington, D.C.: National Science Foundation, 1977.

Armstrong, L. *How to Turn Up Into Down Into Up: A Child's Guide to Inflation, Depression, and Economic Recovery.* New York: Harcourt Brace Jovanovich, 1978.

Barcus, R.E. *Television In the Afternoon Hours.* Newton, Mass.: Action for Children's Television, 1975(a).

Barcus, R.E. *Weekend Commercial Children's Television.* Newton, Mass.: Action for Children's Television, 1975(b).

Cater, D., and Strickland, S. *TV Violence and the Child.* New York: Russell Sage Foundation, 1977.

Comstock, George, et al. *Television and Human Behavior.* New York: Columbia University Press, 1978.

Cook, Thomas D., et al. *Sesame Street Revisited.* New York: Russell Sage Foundation, 1975.

Goldberg, M.E.; Gorn, G.J.; and Givson, W.A. "TV Messages for Snack and Breakfast Foods: Do they Influence Children's Preferences?" *Journal of Consumer Research.* 5, No. 2, 1978.

Guidelines. Princeton, N.J., National Council for Children and Television, 1979.

Gussow, J.D. "Children vs. the Gross National Product." *Nutrition Action* 4, No. 11, 1977.

Potter, Rosemary Lee. "Using TV to Teach Thinking Skills," in *Today's Education,* January, 1972.

Roberts, D.F.; Gibson, W.A.; Christenson, P.; Mooser, L.; and Goldberg, M.E. "Immunizing Children Against Commercial Appeals." Paper presented at the annual meeting of the American Psychological Association, Toronto, Canada, August 30, 1978.

Stein, A.H., and Friedrich, L.K. "Television Content and Young Children's Behavior." *Television and Social Behavior, Reports and Papers,* Vol. II: *Television and Social Learning.* Washington, D.C.: Government Printing Office, 1971.

Sutherland, Zena; Monson, Dianne L.; and Arbuthnot, May Hill. *Children and Books.* 6th Ed. Glenview, Ill.: Scott Foresman, 1981.

Thomas, Marlo; Steinem, Gloria; and Pogrebin, Letty Cottin. *Free to Be–You and Me.* New York: McGraw-Hill, 1974.

U.S. Bureau of the Census. *Statistical Abstracts of the United States: 1981.* Washington, D.C.: Government Printing Office, 1981.

Ward, S., and Wackman, D.B. "Television Advertising and Intrafamily Influence: Children's Purchase Influence Attempts and Parental Yielding." In Ward, S.; Wackman, D.B.; and Wartella, E. *How Children Learn to Buy.* Beverly Hills, Calif.: Sage, 1977.

Sources of Nonsexist Materials

China Books and Periodicals, 95 Fifth Avenue, New York, N.Y. 10003

Educational Activities, Inc., Freeport, N.Y. 11520

Emma Willard Task Force on Education, Box 14229, University Station, Minneapolis, Minn. 55408

The Feminist Press, Box 334, Old Westbury, N.Y. 11568

Feminists on Children's Media, P.O. Box 4375, Grand Central Station, New York, N.Y. 10017

The Free to Be Foundation, 370 Lexington Avenue, New York, N.Y. 10017

Joyful World Press, 468 Belvedere Street, San Francisco, Calif. 94117

KNOW, Inc., Box 86031, Pittsburgh, Pa. 15221

Lollipop Power, P.O. Box 1171, Chapel Hill, N.C. 27514

National Organization for Women, Education Task Force, Anne Grant, 617 49th Street, Brooklyn, N.Y. 11220

New England Free Press, 60 Union Square, Somerville, Mass. 02143

New Seed Press, 1001 Karen Way, Mountain View, Calif. 94040

Resource Center on Sex Roles in Education, National Foundation for the Improvement of Education, National Education Association, 1201 16th Street, N.W., Washington, D.C. 20036

Teachers Rights, National Education Association, 1201 16th Street, N.W., Washington, D.C. 20036

Women's Heritage Series, Box 3236, Santa Monica, Calif. 90403

Unit 4 Mathematics in the Early Elementary Program

OBJECTIVES

After studying this unit, you will be able to

- list and explain the goals of the early elementary mathematics program.
- describe five guidelines for planning mathematical experiences.
- define the following mathematical skills and describe at least two activities to develop each skill: classifying, comparing, ordering (seriation), measurement, geometry, fractions, addition, and subtraction.

As we begin our unit on early elementary mathematics, consider the short scene below, encapsulating a child's mathematical understanding:

Babysitter: Claire, how many hot dogs can you eat?
Claire: I don't know. My mother always makes me stop.

"How many" meant one thing to the child and something else to the babysitter. There are many other times when adults and children are communicating on two different levels about the same thing—one at a child's level of understanding and the other at the adult's level. This is especially true in math.

Too often adults feel that math for young children is what goes on in first grade, doing "real" math problems in workbooks, adding and subtracting at the blackboard. Yet young children learn math ideas quite naturally and happily in everyday life. In the early childhood years, whether in preschool or in the primary grades, children are actively involved in the physical world around them and are naturally curious about number, space, and size. They have a positive feeling about numbers and their uses, and do not see them as "work." Thus math ideas develop quite naturally as young learners move, touch, and manipulate real objects and hear and try new words about these experiences.

In such a way, basic math ideas are formed which become the basis upon which all future math skills will be built in later schooling. In this way, math is not a sit-at-your-desk-with-paper-and-pencil activity, but a part of life.

The young child's attitude toward math is formed to a great degree in the early childhood years. This is why the early childhood teacher's own approach to math needs to be *positive* and *enthusiastic*. This unit will attempt to show how math can be fun for both young children and their teachers.

Included in this unit are the goals of the early elementary mathematics program and suggestions for planning mathematical experiences to develop the skills of classifying, comparing, ordering (seriation), measurement, geometry, fractions, addition, and subtraction. You will find activities for each of these skills included in the discussion of the topic and in the activity section at the end of the unit.

Throughout, the focus is on the pleasure—and not the pain—that is to be related with a young child's learning of math. By using the ideas in this unit in planning experiences for young children, you will help establish the positive attitudes so crucial to a child's learning math.

Because of the wide range of abilities usually present in the early elementary grades, some of the beginning level mathematical activities described may be more appropriate for some children. For example, rote counting, one-to-one correspondence, and numeral recognition skills may be appropriate for many first grade children. Here, as in all curriculum areas, the teacher's knowledge of individual ability levels will be the guide to all activity choices.

GOALS OF THE EARLY ELEMENTARY MATHEMATICS PROGRAM

In learning about mathematics, young children need many chances to interact with objects, many experiences "trying out" ideas, and lots of objects to manipulate physically in order to develop mathematical ideas. To meet these needs, math programs in the primary grades should:

- Provide for individual differences among children: different abilities, learning styles, pace of learning, and interests.
- Be sensitive to the developmental characteristics of young learners, including short attention span and need for *active* learning.
- Include activities that apply math to everyday life.
- Relate math to other learning experiences in school.
- Present basic ideas of math in a form that is not too abstract for the age group.
- Provide appropriate activities for the development of math ideas and skills.

Putting these goals into practice means that the teacher *plans* for specific math ideas to be learned in daily activities. For example, a child may be involved in a cooking activity without understanding the mathematical concepts involved. Applying the program goal of relating math to other learning experiences, the teacher uses the cooking activity to reinforce measurement terms through teacher-child interaction. This interaction is crucial, since the child may measure, for instance, and not associate the word "half" with the measure unless the teacher points out the relationship in the context of the activity. Of course, a teacher would also plan specific lessons around measurement to further enrich the ideas being developed in cooking experiences.

Guidelines for Planning Mathematical Experiences. All mathematical experiences are not incidental, although much learning can occur in unplanned ways. The following are guidelines to consider when planning mathematical experiences for young children:

Whether activities are planned or incidental, keep them brief and repeat them often. Twenty to thirty minutes a day for elementary children is much more effective than longer sessions held less frequently.

In reinforcing basic concepts, always relate activities to real objects. In counting, for instance, count fingers and toes, buttons, blocks, balls, spoons, or whatever you have on hand. By touching objects while counting them, children are helped to realize that they are giving a specific number name to a specific object because it is in a particular position in a sequence which is visible to the child. The ability to *see* and *feel* what is being *said* is essential to young children. The use of real objects also helps them discover the properties of these objects.

Work on mathematical concepts and skills gradually. In learning about numbers, for instance, start with numbers one to three, increase to number five, and add higher numbers in sequence as you perceive that the child is ready for them. But in any number sequence always start the counting with number one.

Like all learning activities for young children, make your math activities enjoyable. Try to start your activities with questions that the child will be able to answer so that she has feelings of success and a sense of "I can do it." Praise each small achievement to encourage sustained and renewed effort. Relate math concepts naturally to everyday activities, such as setting the table for snacks, counting boys and girls for games, or mentioning sizes and shapes in block building.

Above all, be patient. If accomplishment of your program goals seems to come slowly, don't hesitate to repeat the activities over and over again. Look for new twists to keep the child's interest and your own. Try some of the suggested activities at the end of this unit for new approaches to basic math concepts. No matter how small the progress, your efforts will be worthwhile, because a sound and pleasant introduction to mathematical concepts is invaluable to all the child's later mathematical experiences.

From these general suggestions, let us now look at some specific math skills that are taught in the primary grades.

SPECIFIC SKILLS IN THE PRIMARY MATH PROGRAM

The skills discussed in this section are not the only ones, and young children should not be forced to work on these or any others. Math skills are best acquired at the child's own rate as she uses them in daily living. Because of the importance of respecting each child's unique level and rate of development, no grade designations are given for the activities.

In the primary years, young children first learn the basic concepts of number, which are then used in all other math skills, such as adding, subtracting, dividing, and multiplying. Three number processes—classifying, comparing, and ordering—are basic to a child's first understanding of numbers. (Gibb and Castaneda, 1975). These processes, in turn, are related to counting, measurement, and other math skills (Copeland, 1974a).

Classifying. The ability to classify means that a child is able to put things together that are alike and to perform a variety of sorting activities. Classification involves language (speech) understanding as well as an understanding of the basic mathematical idea of grouping. The child must understand the meaning of the words used by the adult giving instructions, such as "alike" and "together," in order to actually "put things together that are alike." Also basic to classification is an understanding of concepts and words for *attributes* (descriptive words like *red* blocks, *square* blocks), *purposes* (things *used for* cooking, playing fire fighter), *position* (on the *center,* the *side*), and *location* (*by, near, around*).

A child first classifies on the basis of *one* attribute. This means that the child can put things together on the basis of *one* characteristic (putting all the *red* blocks together). The child gradually learns to classify according to two common characteristics (putting all the *red, square* blocks together). Through continued experiences exploring objects in the environment, a child can learn to classify with an ever-increasing number of attributes.

Following are some ways to work with young children to help develop their ability to classify.

Classifying Activities
- Talk with children about how things such as toys, food, and clothes are alike and how they are different.

Use not only words of size, shape, and color, but also words that relate to use, location, and position.
- Help children develop vocabulary relevant to their activities (see Units 1 and 2 for suggested ways to develop language skills).
- Use activities to develop the meaning of words and phrases needed in the classifying process, such as "alike," "put together," "belong together," "combine."
- Place objects in a box to be sorted into containers marked by pictures of the objects. Mark room areas by pictures and labels that indicate what activities are allowed there.
- Play classification games like "Pick a Pair": Put out three drawings—two that are identical and one that is obviously different (Example: two cats and a triangle). Say, "Who can pick the two pictures that are just alike?" Make this a fast-paced game, putting down the cards as quickly as children can pick out the two that are alike. Have children sitting in line at a table or in a semicircle on the floor so you can show the pictures to them easily. Gradually make the three pictures more similar.

  Mitten Match: Using wallpaper samples or gift-wrap paper mounted on heavy tagboard, cut out many pairs of mittens, each pair with a different pattern. Put the mittens in a box at the math center and have the children match left and right mittens.
- Paste pictures of beans, macaroni, buttons, and similar small objects onto jars. Have children sort items into the correct jar.
- Photo Match: Take a front-view and back-view photo of each child in your classroom. Mount the photos on oaktag to make them sturdy. Print the initials of the children on the backs. Mix up the photos and place them in a box. The children carefully examine the photos and match front views with back views. They are right if the initials match.

Comparing. This basic math skill involves the ability to see the relationship between two objects, based on a specific attribute (or characteristic). For example, when a child says that one block is "longer than" another, the relationship is based on length. Just as in classifying, it is essential in comparing that children have the relevant vocabulary, such as "big," "little," "taller," and "shorter."

The activities that follow are designed to provide practice in the use of these words and in the skill of comparing.

Comparing Activities

- Select two objects such as blocks or balls that differ only in size. Ask the child which is the bigger ball (or block), then which is the smaller. Have the child physically manipulate the items to compare them. Talk about what they had to do to be sure which was bigger, or smaller.

- Cut out and mount on pieces of cardboard in three distinct sizes three beds and three dolls. Be sure that each item is the same in every way except size. Ask a child to put dolls to bed in the bed that is the right size for each doll. Use other cutouts such as clothes, cars, people, and houses. Use real objects, too, if possible.

- To practice with the concepts of "big" and "little" use toy zoo and farm animals. There should be a big and a little one of each kind of animal. Tell the children that we have big animals (pick up a big or "mama" elephant) and we have little animals ("baby" elephant). Talk about and compare the size of the animals. Next have the children put all of the big animals in one big cage and all of the little animals in a little cage. Present the animals in pairs (one big and one little or one mama or papa and one baby). Show the two animals and ask which one is big and should go in the big cage and which one is little and should go in the little cage. Use the words "big" and "little" often.

- During snack time have the children identify both big and little crackers. Use regular and miniature size candy bars. Compare candy bars of the same brand but different sizes (big and little).

- Palm Trace: Provide a paintbrush and water-soluble paint. Children work in pairs. One child shuts her eyes as the other child traces a number, letter, or geometric shape on her palm with the paint brush. The first child calls out the name of the letter, number, or shape, and then looks to see if she was right. The children switch roles and play again.

- Teepee Shapes. Cut a large, heavy sheet of posterboard into the shape of an Indian teepee. Cut out a variety of shapes from colored construction paper or tagboard. Make duplicates of each shape. Paste one set on the teepee, and put a drapery hook through the top of each shape. Punch a hole in each of the second set of shapes. The children hang each shape on the teepee on the appropriate hook so that the shapes match.

Ordering/Seriation. The skill of ordering involves arranging objects according to some rule or pattern (Gibb and Castaneda, 1975). For example, an ordering task would be to arrange five blocks of different lengths from the longest to the shortest. The rule would be that each block after the first must be shorter than the block it follows.

Again, this skill is related to the child's language development. This means that children should be asked to order objects only on the basis of attributes (or characteristics) they understand. Obviously, a child cannot order blocks from longest to shortest without understanding the words "longest" and "shortest."

This is why in ordering or in any other of the basic math skills, the teacher needs to build the concepts *gradually,* adding new tasks as the child shows understanding of others. The following activities include ways to introduce and practice the math skill of ordering as well as the words used in ordering, such as "first," "middle," and "last."

Ordering Activities

- Help child arrange jar lids, bottles, or fishing weights in order of size. In cooking activities, use different sized glasses as cookie cutters to make cookies or biscuits of graduated sizes.

- Cut paper towel tubes to three different lengths. Help children line them up as stairs. Let children line up each other's shoes from largest to smallest.

- To reinforce the use of the ordering words "first" and "last," have the children stand in a line and identify the person who is first, the person who is last, and even the person in the middle, if possible.

- Show five blocks that have been ordered according to height. Arrange another set of blocks to match the first, third, and fifth blocks in the five-block pattern. Ask the child to put in the two remaining blocks so that both sets match. Repeat, using different children in the group.

- Collect three or more objects in one of the following categories:

Dolls	Nails	Spoons
Trucks	Wood	Forks
Hats	Crayons	Jars
Shoes	Books	Cans
Socks	Coins	Cloth scraps
Necklaces	Pots	Stuffed animals
Pencils	Cups	

Have the children arrange them from largest to smallest, shuffle the objects, and then rearrange them. Let the children try to order the objects without assistance. Help children having difficulty to compare only two objects at a time.

After a few times, change the order and go from smallest to largest.

Variation: Collect a few of the objects in one box. Let the children sort the objects into like groups and then arrange them in order by size.

- Cut out triangles of different sizes such as the same base length but different heights. Select a set of triangles that varies along one dimension. Lay them in front of the child in a mixed order, yet so that the child does not have to turn the triangles to discover the size variation. Have the child order them from smallest to largest (shortest to tallest) or largest to smallest.

When a child can order the triangles, lay them on the floor again, but this time shuffle them so that the child must turn and compare them to arrange them according to height or width.

- Assemble drinking straws, pipe cleaners, or paper towel tubes cut into different lengths. In a small group of children ask a child to arrange the objects in order from longest to shortest or vice versa. Try to let the child do as much as possible. If a mistake is made, use questions to try to get the child to observe the error. Be sure also to ask questions when a correct response is given. Vary the activity by using different materials.

Measurement. In measurement, the goal is to provide young children with many experiences of physically manipulating materials involving volume, weight, and other forms of measurement. More specifically, such activities should include the opportunity to:

- Understand measuring as a way of answering questions, such as "How much?" or "How far?"
- Understand that measuring requires the use of some unit (foot ruler, yardstick, piece of string) that can be used over and over again.
- Use scales, calendar, stopwatch, meterstick, cup, and other measuring tools to solve problems that are meaningful to the child.

The following activities are designed to help young children *actively* learn about measuring.

Measurement Activities
- Cooking activities provide excellent practice in measurement.
- Activities involving water, sand, clay, beans, and other liquids and particles concretely show that the quantity of a given unit is constant. These activities are good for teaching number, weight, and volume. Experiment filling different sizes of containers with the same quantity of material for this concrete, visual experience with measurement concepts.
- With young children, use vocabulary related to weight, temperature, time, money, size, capacity, and distance, such as the following:

Measure	Short	High
Big	Wide	Hole
Fat	Deep	Pound
Tiny	Low	Ruler

FIGURE 4–1 Cooking is a good activity to practice the math skill of measurement.

Teaspoon	Square	Minute
Tablespoon	Cube	Buy
Cup	Cone	Sell
Quart	Triangle	Penny
Pint	Thermometer	Nickel
Speedometer	Clock	Dollar
Round	Hour	Scales
Circle		

Note: Do not confuse the children by introducing standard weights and measures and their metric equivalent at the same time, even though they may use metrics later in their educational experiences.

- Have the children find items in the room of specific lengths. Next, have them draw these on a piece of paper and write down their lengths. They will have to measure numerous things before locating an item of the specified length.
- Use rulers and yardsticks in the woodworking center.
- Model measurement activities. Measure the distance a child runs, jumps, or throws a ball. Measure and record the children's heights.
- Post a large calendar and fill in the dates squares with upcoming events. Every day discuss the day, date, and special events.
- Ask questions requiring clock use with words such as "hour," "minute," etc. Ask questions such as: "What time is lunch?" "What time do you go home?" "What time do you get up?"
- Plan special lessons to develop measurement ideas, such as the one in Figure 4–2 on telling time. This lesson combines the math skill of measurement with a movement activity.

Geometry. Basic skills in geometry for young children involve the ability to recognize and identify shapes such as squares, triangles, circles, and rectangles. The ability to tell the difference between shapes is also a basic reading skill.

Making patterns with parquet sets of different shapes and colors is an excellent way to develop the child's understanding of geometric shapes. Also, you can make practice with geometric skills a daily event by pointing out geometric properties of things with which a child is familiar: "Look at the square cracker," "Pick up all the rectangular blocks first," or "I'm thinking of a circle in the art center. . ."

A. Title: Telling Time With Your Body
B. Objective: Telling time
C. Procedure:
1. Discuss the clock: the large (minute) hand, small (hour) hand, and the numbers.
2. Directions to the children:
   a. The upper part of your body can be the hour hand.
   b. The lower part of your body can be the minute hand.
   c. The numbers of the clock are on the floor or on a chart on the wall.

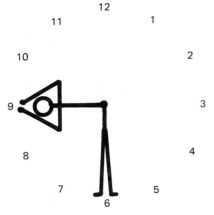

   d. After the teacher announces the time, you will use your body like the hands of a clock.
   e. One child will be the teacher and announce the time to be made.
3. Examples:
   a. 12 o'clock—in a sitting position with head, hands, and feet at twelve and seat in the center.
   b. 3:30—side position, head and hands directed toward three and feet at six.
   c. 9:30—side position, head and hands directed toward nine and feet at six.

FIGURE 4–2 Sample lesson plan: measurement

Discovering geometric properties of familiar objects in this way also helps a child's development of other basic math skills. For example, she may compare and classify objects according to geometric characteristics.

FIGURE 4-3 Learning to recognize the difference in shapes is the beginning of geometry. Tracing shapes is a good related activity.

A. Title: Snack Shape Matchup
B. Objective: Recognize circle, triangle, square
C. Materials: Cutouts of a circle, triangle, and square; varied snack crackers and cookies in these shapes. (Ritz crackers, Cheezits, Sociables, Doritos)
D. Procedure:
  1. On the first day plan *one* shaped snack
  2. Present cutouts of shapes to children. Compare the shapes of the cutouts with that of the snack for the day.
  3. Have one child match the snack to the cutout of the same shape.
  4. On another day present several snacks of different shapes on a tray.
  5. Children are to take two that are the same.

FIGURE 4-4 Math activity: geometric shapes

Here, too, the child's level of language development must be taken into account if these activities are to be meaningful.

In the example in Figure 4-4, a teacher used a daily activity (snack time) to reinforce geometric shapes.

The following activities suggest ways to work with young children on geometric shapes.

Geometry Activities
- Cut shapes of triangles, squares, and circles from styrofoam packing trays. Punch a hole in the middle for stringing on a shoestring. Use in sorting and matching activities.
- Have triangular, square, and circular beanbags, which must be put through the correctly shaped hole in a shoebox. Have children glue macaroni, beans, or pebbles to cutouts of geometric shapes and use them for the same activity.
- Have templates (or cutouts) of triangles, squares, and circles which children can trace. Have building blocks of the various shapes. Have heavily outlined triangles, squares, and circles for coloring.

- Play games like "The Mystery Box": Use a box or bag and geometric shapes of various types of material. (The kindergartens should have parquetry shapes that would be excellent for this activity, also wooden letter shapes.) Place the shapes in a "feel" box, or a cardboard box with a hole cut into the top. The child must reach in, feel the object, and identify its shape by touch. She may then remove the object to see if she guessed correctly. This can be done with the children seated in a circle on the floor.
- Use geometric shapes with movement education activities such as "The Geometric Shape Crawl": Spread large geometric shapes cut out of cardboard around the floor. Challenge the children to crawl between the shapes, naming each shape before they can crawl past it. Try other challenges like "Can you crawl through without touching the sides?"
- The Shadow Design Game: Use an opaque projector, movie projector, or other light source. Aim the light against a wall, and have a child step in front of the light creating shadows. Give the child movement directions using mathematical words such as: "Make your shadow as big (or as small) as you can." "How tall (or short) can you make your shadow?" "Can you make your shadow very wide?"

Fractions. Very early in life young children use basic fractional concepts. For example, a child understands that an apple or a banana can be divided into parts.

The number of pieces in the whole can give the child the name for the fraction. For example, an apple divided into four pieces leads to the name "fourths." Of course, children will need to understand ordinal (order) names before learning the names of fractions. For example, they will need to understand the words "third" and "fourth" before they can understand these fractional parts.

The teaching suggestions below are designed to help you introduce and practice fractions in various activities.

Fractions Activities
- Use fractional words regularly in daily activities, such as one-half of the group, half a cup of milk, *divide* the papers, a *piece* of the apple.
- Use fractional words as you encourage sharing: "half an apple," "a whole cookie," "half a sandwich."
- Use fractional vocabulary in comparing blocks and other objects: "half as big," "half as long."
- Prepare pudding, jello, and other foods using measuring spoons and cups.
- Have the children cut pictures into two to four pieces, then paste them back together. Cut simple shapes or objects (clothing articles, ice cream cones, apples, animals) out of construction paper. Trace their outlines on white paper with magic marker. Then cut the objects in half. Have the child paste the two halves onto the outline.
- Have children match up halves of common objects which are cut or broken in half (pencils, plastic eggs, styrofoam trays, empty spools, plastic lids, old clothing articles). Give each of several children one-half of a different object. Place the other halves of the objects in a pile in front of the children. Each child is to find the other half of her object as quickly as possible.
- Use colored plastic Easter eggs which come apart and have children put them together by matching color. Or using plastic egg-shaped panty hose containers, place a piece of candy or other surprise inside. Have children open to find surprise, then put parts back together.

- Cut small distinct boxes (pudding, cereal, perfume) in half. Have children help you match halves.

Addition. Addition is the mathematical skill of combining numbers (or addends) to get a sum (or total). The activities under this heading are intended to supplement a textbook, not to replace it. These activities are designed to provide addition fact practice.

It is important to encourage the children to count when confirming a response to an addition exercise. It is also important to reinforce one-to-one correspondence when counting. Further, children should be allowed to use objects and materials to count on as long as necessary when working addition problems.

A special note is necessary on working with an addend of zero. Initial work with addition should avoid this special case of an "empty" set. The early elementary child needs concrete objects for mathematical understanding, and since the empty set contains no objects most learners at this level cannot yet work with it. The teacher should make sure that children have successfully experienced addition without zero before including addition with the zero. Different textbooks introduce work with zero at different points in the curriculum, and the teacher should take special note of its placement and plan activities accordingly.

Addition Activities
- Duck Families: Make cutouts of large ("mother") ducks, each marked with a numeral from 1 to 5. Make cutouts of small ("baby") ducks each marked with a possible addition combination for the number on the mother duck (for example, the 5 combinations would be 4 + 1, 1 + 4, 3 + 2, 2 + 3, 5 + 0, and 0 + 5).

  In a group of two to four children, have each child select a mother duck. Then have the child find all the baby ducks that have an addition fact that appears on the mother duck.

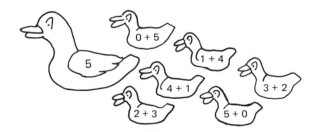

- Daisies: Make large daisy petals, each with an addition problem on it. Make daisy centers with the corresponding sums.

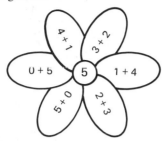

In a small group of two to four children, have the children match the problems (petals) to the correct sums (centers). Petals can be color coded on the back for checking answers: All the petals for the number 5 could be marked red, all those for 4 could be green, and so on.

- Pouch Problems: On a large cardboard kangaroo staple pockets, each marked with a number from 1 to 9. On cards, write addition facts for the sum on each of the pockets.

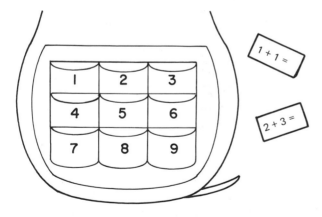

In a small group of one or two children, have the children choose a card and place it in the pocket that shows the correct sum.

Variation: Numbers and problems can be made more difficult as children become adept at old problems.

- Problem Puzzle: Make a gameboard with addition problems scattered on it randomly. Next cut the gameboard into pieces, separating each problem from its answer.

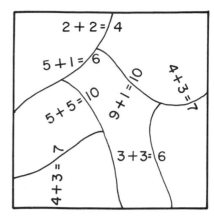

The children must put the problems together to reassemble the puzzle. The level of difficulty should be consistent with the children's ability. Any kind of problem—subtraction, addition, or multiplication—can be used.

Subtraction. It seems to be popular in many early elementary textbooks to present subtraction facts as the "opposite" of addition facts. Proponents of this approach justify their viewpoint by claiming that it gives children a better understanding of both operations. However, children's math performance has not proven their case. It seems that before a relationship between these two mathematical processes can be well understood, each of the processes must be understood separately by the child.

Subtraction facts should be introduced with modeled activities similar to those used with addition. At the beginning, subtraction facts should be taught using real world examples, demonstrated with objects. The facts will eventually become mentally internalized through practice. After a child learns the subtraction facts involving numbers to five, it may be wise to develop the relationship of addition and subtraction.

The mathematical process of subtraction involves a *minuend,* a *subtrahend,* and a *difference.* For example, in the problem $5 - 3 = 2$, the number 5 is the minuend, 3 is the subtrahend, and 2 is the difference.

Subtraction facts with minuends through 5 should be learned first, then minuends through 10, and last minuends through 18. The special case of subtracting zero should be introduced when your textbook series introduces it. The difficulty of working with a set of zero has been discussed. Despite the difficulty, realizing that the problem exists puts the teacher a step ahead. The reasonable remedy seems to be to delay work with zero until the child has had some successful experience with initial subtraction problems.

In addition to the following subtraction activities, the teacher should review the addition activities to determine which could be used with subtraction problems, too.

Subtraction Activities

• Match the Socks: Cut out pairs of tagboard socks, each pair showing a subtraction problem and its answer. Have children sort the socks, clipping each problem with a spring-type clothespin or paper clip to the correct answer.

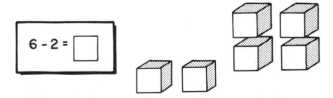

• Count Encounters: Give each child 10 inch cubes. Two children sit facing each other with a card deck of subtraction facts (minuend of 10 or less). One child turns over the top card on the deck and the other child works the problem. In working the problem, the child may use the cubes to generate the fact or recall it from memory. If correct, the child keeps the card; if incorrect, the card is returned to the deck.

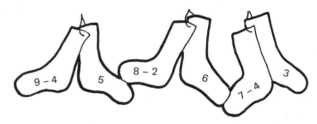

• Subtraction Fish: Use pairs of cards, a subtraction sentence on one card and the correct answer on the other. In a small group of two to six children, shuffle the cards and deal five to each player. Spread the remaining cards face down in a "pool" in the middle of the group. Each child takes a turn drawing a fish

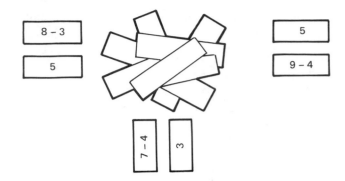

from the pool and tries to make a pair. If a pair can be made, the player lays the cards face up; if not, the player must return one card to the pool. The winner is the player with the most pairs when all plays have been made.

• Spot the Leopard: Use a spotted leopard as illustrated, and circular playing cards, the same size as the leopard's spots, showing subtraction problems.

Number the spots on the leopard to correspond with the correct answers to the subtraction problems. Deal an equal number of spot cards to each player; set aside the remainder. Taking turns, players try to match their problem spots to the correct answer spots on the leopard. If a player places a spot incorrectly, it must be taken back and the player loses a turn. The winner is the first player to place all her spots correctly.

In order to be sure that there is a place, time, and appropriate materials for the kinds of math activities that help children grow in their understanding of mathematical

---

GOALS OF THE CENTER

- Using numbers
- Developing quantitative concepts

- Enumerating real objects
- Tactile, visual, and auditory counting

Materials

Scales
Thermometers
Tape measures, metersticks, rulers
Measuring spoons and cups
Counters (blocks, beads, sticks, straws, buttons,
    snap clothespins, bottle caps)
Math books (library or textbooks)
Games (commercial, teacher-made, or student-made)
Balances
Puzzles
Playing cards
Bead frame (abacus)
Cuisenaire rods
Number lines (on display and individual)
Play money and cash register

Clocks
Worksheets in plastic envelopes
Geoboards
Flannel board
Magnetic board and numbers
Flashcards
Dominoes
Pegboards
Attribute blocks
Problem cards
Dice
Pattern blocks
Unifix cubes (plastic attachable cubes in varied
    colors)

FIGURE 4–5 Math center

concepts, a teacher needs to set up a math center in the room. Figure 4–5 lists some basic math materials for an early elementary math center.

SUMMARY

In the early elementary years young children learn basic math skills that they will use all through school. This is why it is so important that their early experiences with math be positive. For this to be so, young children must have many active learning experiences in basic math skills in a relaxed atmosphere and at their own level of ability and interest.

These learning experiences offer young children the chance to develop simple understandings that later unfold as the child meets more and more math challenges in later school years. In our next unit we will see how to present basic math skills in still other ways.

LEARNING ACTIVITIES

A. Using a school supply catalog, choose three pieces of math equipment appropriate for teaching each of the following skills:

- Seriation
- Geometric shapes
- Addition
- Subtraction
- Classification

B. Imagine that as a teacher of a first grade you have $75 to spend on math equipment. Using a school supply catalog, spend this sum for your class. Explain

1. What you bought.
2. Developmental reason for choice.
3. Purpose(s) of item.

C. Choose one of the addition activities from the unit. Develop any necessary materials for the activity.

Then use the activity with a small group of children. Evaluate your experience. Share your results with your classmates.

D. Think of additional activities for teaching one of the mathematical skills in this unit.

E. Visit a classroom and observe a mathematics activity. Evaluate the activity. Was it appropriate for the age of the children? For their abilities? Would you have made any changes in the activity? Was the activity effective? Why or why not?

F. Visit a children's library and choose at least three children's books to use as part of a unit on mathe- matics. Bring the books to class. What number concepts are taught by the books? How would you use the books with children? How effective would the books be in teaching number concepts to children?

G. Plan a cooking activity for a small group of children to reinforce the mathematical concept of fractions. Make a chart to use with the cooking activity. Then conduct the activity with a small group of children and evaluate your experience. Share the results with your classmates.

ACTIVITIES FOR CHILDREN

Snail Trail

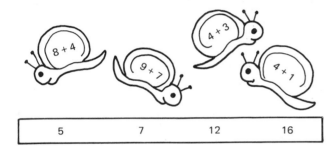

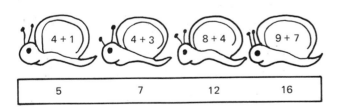

A. Using tagboard or heavy construction paper, make a number of snails and label each with an addition or subtraction computation problem. You may put the answers on the backs of the snails, under flaps if you wish, for self-checking.

B. Now make a number of snail trails, randomly placing the answers to the snail problems along the trails.

C. The child puts a snail trail on the floor or table, finds the snails that match that trail, and places each snail at its appropriate location on the trail.

Catch the Worm

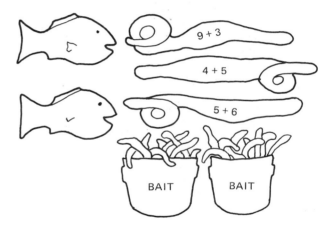

A. Cut out two fish, using heavy tagboard; laminate them so that they will be durable. Put them in an envelope.

B. Cut out many worm shapes, using heavy tagboard. Write an addition or subtraction computation on each worm, and put the answer on the back. Laminate the worms, also, and put them in a box.

C. Provide two bait cans.

D. Two children may play this game. They flip a coin to see who goes first.

E. The first player randomly selects a worm from the box and places the worm next to her fish. If she can solve the computation problem on the worm, the worm goes into her bait can. If the problem is solved incor- rectly, the child must leave the worm out on the table.

F. The children continue in turn until there are no more worms in the box. The child who has the most worms in her bait can is the winner.

Ladybug Game Board

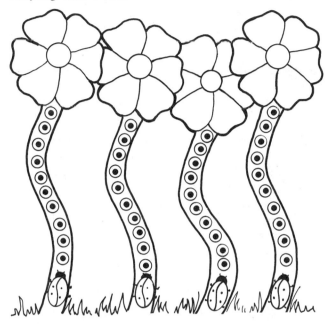

A. Cut out four large, colorful flowers and four green stems, and glue them to heavy tagboard. Glue 10 small, metal washers, about 2 inches apart, along each flower stem and one to the center of the flower. Provide four magnetized ladybugs. Prepare a set of about 50 addition and subtraction computation problems on index cards.

B. Four children play. They take turns picking a computation problem from the deck of index cards. They check their answers on the backs of the cards.

C. If the child gets the problem correct, she moves her magnetized ladybug ahead one washer.

D. If she gives an incorrect answer, she stays where she is, places the card at the bottom of the pile, and waits for her next turn.

E. The play continues until one child gets a ladybug to the center of the flower.

Catch the Fly

A. Using heavy tagboard or durable construction paper, cut out frogs, flies, and 15 to 20 lily pads. Write an

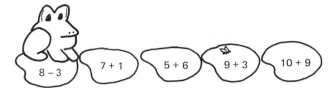

addition or subtraction computation problem on each lily pad. Put the answers on the backs.

B. The child places the lily pads in a row on the floor or table. The frog is placed on the first lily pad and the fly on the fourth lily pad. The object of the game is to get the fly to the end of the row before it is captured by the frog.

C. The child answers the arithmetic problem on the fifth lily pad, and checks the answer on the back of the pad. If correct, the child moves the fly to that pad. The frog also moves ahead one lily pad. The child goes on to the problem on the next lily pad.

D. If, however, the child's answer was incorrect, she moves the frog one lily pad ahead but leaves the fly where it was.

E. The child goes on to try the problem on the next pad. The frog moves ahead one lily pad at every turn. Since the fly moves ahead one lily pad only when the child gives the correct answer, the frog will catch up with the fly if she misses three problems. This will indicate that more direct teaching is needed for this child.

Mushroom Match

A. Cut mushroom shapes out of construction paper and laminate them. Write an addition or subtraction computation on the top half, and the answer on the bottom half. Cut apart the tops of the mushrooms from the stems.

B. Place all the problems in one box and all the answers in another box.

C. The children are to match the tops and bottoms to make correct problem-answer combinations. They check the backs of the mushroom tops to see if their solutions are correct.

UNIT REVIEW

1. What is most important about a teacher's approach to teaching mathematics to young children?
2. Describe five guidelines to follow when planning mathematical activities for the child in the early elementary grades?
3. List the goals of the early elementary level mathematics program and give an example of activities for each goal.
4. Define "classifying." What appropriate activities would you plan to reinforce this skill?
5. Define ordering (seriation). Describe activities which would be appropriate for teaching this skill.
6. Define addition and subtraction skills. What kinds of activities would be appropriate for teaching these skills? Give at least two examples for each skill.
7. When should addition and subtraction problems involve zero? Why is it important to be careful about introducing zero in math problems for early elementary level children?
8. How can geometry skills be incorporated into activities at the early elementary grade levels? Give two examples of geometry activities.
9. How can introductory information on fractions be incorporated into activities for early elementary level children? Give at least two examples of these activities.
10. Give two examples of activities for reinforcing measurement skills in the early elementary grades.

ADDITIONAL READINGS

Copeland, Richard W. *Diagnostic and Learning Activities In Mathematics for Children.* New York: Macmillan, 1974(a).

Copeland, Richard W. *How Children Learn Mathematics: Teaching Implications of Piaget's Research.* New York: Macmillan, 1974(b).

Gibb, Glenadine, and Castaneda, Alberta M. "Experiences for Young Children." In J.N. Payne, (ed.) *Mathematics Learning In Early Childhood.* Reston, Va.: National Council of Teachers of Mathematics, 1975.

Moursund, David G., and Shutt, Douglas L. *Calculators in the Classroom.* New York: John Wiley, 1981.

Nichols, Eugene D., and Behr, Merlyn J. *Elementary School Mathematics and How to Teach It.* New York: Holt, Rinehart and Winston, 1982.

Paige, Donald D.; Thiessen, Diane; and Wild, Margaret. *Elementary Mathematical Methods,* 2nd Ed. New York: John Wiley, 1982.

Richardson, Lloyd I.; Goodman, Kathy L.; Hartman, Nancy; and LePique, Henri C. *A Mathematics Activity Curriculum for Early Childhood and Special Education.* New York: Macmillan, 1980.

Silverman, Helene and Sheila. *Your Days are Numbered in Calendar Math.* New Rochelle, N.Y.: Cuisenaire Co. of America, 1981.

Unit 5 Mathematics Activities

OBJECTIVES

After studying this unit, you will be able to

- describe at least three activities for teaching addition and subtraction skills at the early elementary level.
- describe at least three activities each for teaching classifying, comparing, and ordering skills.
- describe at least three activities each for teaching measurement, geometry, and fractions.

As we saw in Unit 4, it is important to provide young elementary students with many and varied opportunities to be *actively* involved in learning mathematical skills. To assist teachers in providing these varied experiences, this unit contains additional activity suggestions. These activities are organized in the same order they are presented in Unit 4: classifying, comparing, ordering (seriation), measurement, geometry, fractions, addition, and subtraction.

The math activities in this section are designed to make math a creative experience for young children in the early elementary years. They are just a beginning. Let your own and the children's interests and needs be the guide to many, many more creative math experiences.

Have fun trying these activities and discovering the positive learning experiences that math can provide.

CLASSIFYING

- Talk about how objects such as furniture, clothes, books, etc. are alike and how they are different. Include not only words of size, shape, and color, but also words that relate to use, location, and position.
- Use activities to develop meaning for words and phrases used in the classifying process, such as "alike," "put together," "belong together," "combine."
- Have shoeboxes of collected objects, such as beads, buttons, seeds, nails, blocks, felt shapes, and checkers. Do not use all the objects each time you take the boxes out. Make a selection each time. Ask the child to find two objects that are the same. Talk about how the objects are the same. Pick out one object and ask the child to find another object that is the same in at least one way. Repeat, using two objects.

- Make a collection of felt cutouts using a variety of shapes, sizes, and colors. Ask children to put together cutouts that are alike in some way or that are the same. Discuss. Repeat, using other objects that can be sorted such as buttons, washers, blocks, nails, toys, cups, and spoons.
- Ask the child to select two objects that are in some way the same. Ask other children to guess how the two objects are the same. Repeat, using books, furniture, etc.
- Using the collections suggested, select one object, such as a block. Ask a child to start a set with it. Have the child name the set and select other members of the set.

COMPARING

Short and Tall Matchup. Divide the children into groups of three. Try to have all three children in each group of different heights. One child is designated the "referee"; the other two stand back to back. The referee decides which of the other two is short and which is tall. After children in the other groups have checked the referee's decision, another child in each group becomes the referee. Continue until all children have had a chance to be referee.

Nature's Comparisons
A. Equipment: A collection of seeds, potting soil, and empty milk cartons.
B. Procedure: Let the children plant their own seeds. Every day have the children check on the progress of their seeds. As the plants grow, discuss how the plants are changing. Young children may have difficulty

doing this so you may want to take pictures of the seedlings that show their growth. You might also want to cut a piece of adding-machine tape the same length as the plant and keep a graph of the growth on the bulletin board.

Thread and Rope
A. Equipment: Thread, string, and rope of different thicknesses.
B. Procedure: Show the children two pieces of thread, string, or rope (use two different thicknesses); ask or tell the children which is thick and which is thin. Have them identify which is which. Then ask them, "If I wanted to sew on a button, which piece would I use, the thick one or the thin one?" Then ask, "If we were going to play tug-of-war, which piece would we use, the thick one or the thin one?" Repeat with other pairs of thread, string, and rope, using similar questions; or let the children ask the questions.

Stripes
A. Equipment: Tempera paint, wide and narrow paint brushes, paper, and felt-tipped pens.
B. Procedure: Tell the children that they are going to design some clothes with stripes. Draw a garment and show them how it can be painted with wide stripes or narrow stripes or both.

Let each child outline a garment (or you can do it for them with a marker) and then paint stripes on it. Have each child tell you whether each of the stripes is narrow or wide.

When the garments are dry, cut them out and post them; have a fashion show on your wall or bulletin board.

Space Game. One child is "it." The others form two lines, hands joined, facing each other with a narrow corridor between them. It stands at one end of the corridor and tries to walk, run, or crawl through the tunnel when you give the "go" signal.

As it is proceeding, call out "wide space!" at which the two lines back apart, making its progress easier, or "narrow space!" at which the two lines quickly walk toward each other, stopping it.

Before playing the game, stress that everyone is to move carefully so as not to bump into each other when making a narrow space. The child who is it should "freeze" when the corridor becomes too narrow.

Can You Find?
A. Equipment: Rods, common objects in the room.
B. Procedure: Give each of the children a rod. Ask, "Can you find something in this room that is longer than your rod?" Demonstrate with your rod, if necessary. After all the children have found something longer than their rods, ask them if they can find something shorter than their rods.

ORDERING/SERIATION

Yummy Lengths
A. Equipment: Cardboard cutouts of hot dogs and buns, in different lengths. Make each hot dog so that it fits exactly into its own bun.
B. Procedure: Have the child arrange the hot dogs in order of length. Then instruct the child to sequence the buns in the same order, so that each hot dog matches its own bun. To check, have the child put the hot dogs in the buns. Be sure to check beforehand to be certain the dogs match the buns exactly.

Jumping in Lengths
A. Equipment: Long string, scissors, masking tape, and pen.
B. Procedure: Lay the string out on the floor in a straight line. Have each child take a turn jumping as far as possible along the string (specify jumping with feet together or apart). Record the jump by cutting that length of string and marking it with the child's name on masking tape. When the jumping is over, let small groups of children compare their lengths of string and order them from longest to shortest. The whole class may order their strings from shortest to longest. Save the strings and repeat at a later time in the year. Compare the old jump with the new one.

Ribbons in Order
A. Equipment: Ribbons of the same length but of different widths.
B. Procedure: Have the child arrange the ribbons in order from the widest to the narrowest. Let the children try this by themselves once they get the idea of what to do.

Art Collages. Provide the children with three or four different items (such as pieces of straws, circles, pieces of spaghetti, circle stickers of various sizes). The children make collages by pasting the items on pieces of tagboard or cardboard.

Make button collages with many sizes of buttons pasted onto styrofoam meat trays.

String various lengths of straws.

Make box sculpture with boxes of various sizes pasted together, allowed to dry, and then decorated.

Make a spaghetti collage. Cut spaghetti into various lengths, cook it, and then drain it. Rinse the spaghetti in cool water. Varied lengths of spaghetti are put on colored paper in designs. Cooked spaghetti has enough starch to act as a glue.

Use pictures of objects or animals ordered from smallest to largest to make collages.

In all of these art activities, reinforce the concepts of ordering by using such words as "largest," "smallest," "smaller," "thinner," "thinnest," etc.

Mirrors and Size. Place mirrors at three different levels so that the children will have to position themselves at different levels to see themselves. One mirror should be very low, one at about the children's level, and one so high that they have to climb up on a chair to reach it.

Ask the child to discriminate between highest and lowest.

Ask the children to tell what they did to become higher and what they did to become lower.

MEASUREMENT

- Ask the children questions about size and discuss various measuring instruments. Let the children handle measuring instruments such as a ruler, yardstick, tape measure, etc.
- Let the child play with a ruler and a yardstick. Ask the child to measure and tell you how many yardsticks long or high the bookcase or the table is.
- Have the child estimate how many small glasses are in a quart and then actually measure and see how close her estimate was.
- Use many water-play and sand-play activities that call for weighing and measuring. Have children use measuring cups and spoons. Point out the various sizes and their related names for the children as they use them.

- Post a large thermometer in the room and call the children's attention to it. Check and record temperatures on the calendar periodically.
- Bring a bathroom scale to class and let the children weigh themselves. Write the child's weight on a card so the child can see it written down. Do this periodically and note the child's growth.
- Show the children a yardstick or measuring tape. Show them how long one inch is. Measure each child and tell him how many inches tall he is. Show him on the wall or on the yardstick. Write the child's height on a card so he can see the information written down. Check periodically and record the child's growth.

GEOMETRY

Patterns of Shapes. Arrange blocks, tiles, or squares of paper of two colors in various patterns (very simple ones at first). The child then duplicates the patterns you have made. Also allow the child time to play freely with the materials. The child needs some time to get the feel of the exercise and explore its potential. When the child has learned to copy simple patterns, he is given a drawing of a pattern to follow. Finally, he can learn to extend patterns by repeating the established pattern. For example, if you start a pattern of two red squares, one white triangle, two red squares, and one white triangle, the child should be able to place additional colored shapes in the same sequence.

Folding in Shapes. Give each child a square or rectangular piece of paper (not construction or heavy paper), and challenge the child to fold it into various shapes.

Shape Bulletin Board. Attach shapes to the bulletin board, with a small container below each shape. Have children match loose identical shapes with those on the board, then drop them into the containers.

Silhouette Identification. Outlines of various shapes (simple shapes such as umbrella, shoe, chair, fish; more complex shapes such as different shapes of shoes, animals, flowers, etc.) are displayed for identification.

Geometric Relay

a. Provide five large tagboard shapes and give small tagboard shapes. There should be enough small shapes for each child to have two.

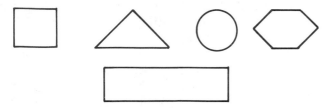

Note to teacher: Distribute to each child a small tagboard shape. Place the patterns of the large shapes 30 to 40 feet in front of each squad. On the signal, have the children who are first on each squad run to his large patterns and place the smaller one on top of the matching large figure. The first squad to do this correctly and return to its original position wins.

Variation: Child could run, hop, or skip around his or her individual shape.

Shape Hopscotch. Form circles, squares, triangles, and other shapes—as you discuss them—with plastic tape on the classroom floor. Then ask each child to find the shapes on the floor. Say: "I'm thinking of a rectangle in the science corner." Ask the children to find other things in the room that are the same shape as the plastic shapes on the floor, such as blocks, panes of glass in the window, etc.

Shape Game

A. Equipment: Geometric shapes are placed on the floor or taped. Choose three shapes and make a large and a small size of each. (If you are outside, you can draw shapes with shoe polish.) Provide task card questions for each shape.

B. Procedure: Have children complete the circuit of shapes, making sure they have visited each one. Examples of questions to ask the children:

- Can you hop around the circle ten times?
- Can you jump over the circle four times?
- Can you jump in the circle two times?
- Can you walk around the circle in your sock feet, feeling the shape with your toes?
- Can you trace the shape with your finger?
- Can you make yourself small inside the shape?

FRACTIONS

Body Fractions. Instead of using imaginary pizza pieces and fearsome looking fraction lines to introduce fraction study, get the kids excited about the subject by helping them discover the fractional parts of their own bodies. Working with a partner, each child cuts a piece of string roughly the same length as the other's height. Have them fold their strings in half to measure body parts that they estimate would be about half their height. (Hips to toes and arm lengths are typical first tries.)

The children can find other fractions by folding their strings into thirds, fourths, and fifths to measure smaller body parts, such as wrists, ankles, knees, and necks. Some children might even continue the folding to measure finger lengths and thumb widths. When done, the students record all their findings on charts divided into columns labeled: 1/2 My Height, 1/3 My Height, 1/4 My Height, and so on. As a lighthearted wrap-up, the kids can measure grins.

After the children acquire a firm understanding of the fraction concept, ease into the number equivalents by having them remeasure their heights and body parts with tape measures and convert the string measures on their charts to inches.

Introduction to 1/2

A. Equipment: Construction paper, magic markers, paste, scissors.

B. Procedure: Cut simple circles of various sizes out of construction paper. Trace the outline of one circle on a white sheet of paper with a magic marker. Cut the circle into two large pieces. Then have the child paste the pieces onto the outline.

C. Variations: Let the children create their own objects from paper and material scraps and cut them up.

Let children cut pictures into two to four pieces and then paste them back together.

Object Matchup

A. Equipment: Several commonplace objects cut or broken in half (pencils, plastic pantyhose eggs, styrofoam trays, empty spools, plastic lids). Use objects that are different in color, texture, and shape.

B. Procedure: Give each of several children one-half of a different object. Place the other halves in a pile in front of the children. Each child is to find the other half of his object as quickly as possible.

C. Variations: This can also be done with colored, plastic Easter eggs which come apart. Children can put the eggs together by matching color.

You might place a piece of candy or other surprise inside.

Have interlocking toys—pop beads, lego blocks, plastic bricks—in the play area.

Make a Shape

A. Equipment: Two circles 6″ in diameter cut out of posterboard. One circle should be cut in half.

B. Procedure: Show the child the whole circle. Take the two pieces of the other circle and place them together to form a whole. Present the two pieces to the child so that they only have to be brought together to form a whole.

Say to the child, "can you put these together to look like this one?" pointing to the whole. After a successful attempt, take the two pieces and turn them to different anlges; ask the child again to put the pieces together to make a shape like the whole.

If the child has difficulty, the whole can be used as an outline and the two pieces matched on top of it.

Remove the whole circle from view. Place the circle half edges parallel to the table top.

Demonstrate putting the pieces together to form a circle. Then replace the pieces at the edge of the table. Ask the child to make a circle with the pieces.

C. Variations: This activity can be done with other shapes (hearts, circles, six-pointed stars) cut from construction paper.

You might also present picture puzzles divided along straight lines to be matched up.

ADDITION

Number Please. You can help children sharpen their addition and graphing skills with the use of an inexpensive, yet abundant, resource—old telephone books. Distribute different pages from an outdated directory to pairs of children. Partners begin by underlining 40 telephone numbers. First, they add the last two digits in each of the 40 numbers (for example: 874–7185; 8 plus 5 equals 13) and then construct a tally sheet showing how many of each sum (from 0 to 18) they find. One partner uses the information to plot a bar graph; the other, a line graph. Each checks the other's work for accuracy.

Bean Bag Clown

A. Equipment: Two bean bags and a face target as shown.

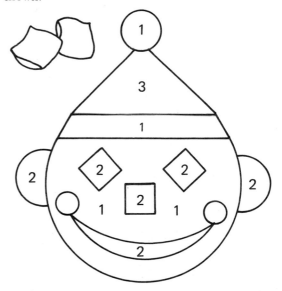

B. Procedure: Each child takes a turn throwing both bean bags at the clown face. The child then finds the sum of the two numbers he hit. If a bean bag lands on a line, the player may choose which of the two numbers to use in the sum. If the sum is correct, the player gets a point.

Sum Eggs

A. Equipment: Plastic eggs, small beads or chips, ditto worksheets, chalkboard or chart paper.

B. Procedure: Fill each egg beforehand with the same number of beads; for example, five. Give each child an egg, and tell the group that you want to find as many ways to make the sum of 5 as you can. Let each child try dividing his beads between the egg halves and telling the combination. Record combinations on a class chart and individual ditto sheets.

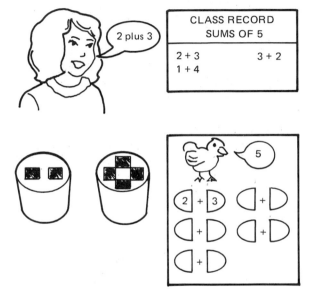

Math Relay

A. Equipment: A numbered grid on the floor or black-top for each group

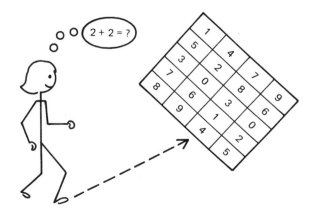

B. Procedure: Divide children into two or three groups. Place a numbered grid on the floor and have the children sit around it while you explain the game to them. Then place a grid in front of each squad. Say: "I will hold up a card with a problem written on it such as 2 + 2 = ?" (You may call out the problems verbally for more advanced students.) "The first child runs and stands in the correct answer. After I check each answer, you will run, hop, or skip back. The team with the most correct answers wins!"

Ring Toss (grades 1–3)

A. Equipment: Use empty plastic (gallon-size) bottles and rubber jar rings, or a commercial ring toss game.

B. Procedure: Children throw rings at the target. Assign points to each of the bottles—highest points for bottles farthest away. Have other children in the group keep score.

Bunny Hop

A. Equipment: Make a bunny, as shown, the size of a hopscotch grid.

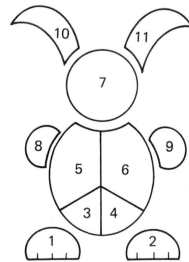

B. Procedure: Ask the children:

- Can you hop from space to space on the bunny?
- Can you hop from space to space only on the even numbers?
- Can you hop from space to space only on the odd numbers?

- Can you throw the beanbag on two numbers that give you the sum of 7?
- Can you throw the beanbag on two numbers that give you the sum of 3?
- Can you throw the beanbag on the largest number?
- Can you throw the beanbag on the smallest number?

Number Baseball

A. Equipment: A baseball gameboard, flashcards with addition problems to sums of 10, game markers, timer or watch with a second hand.

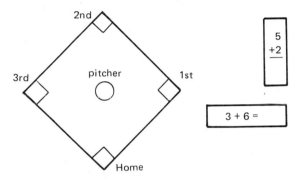

B. Procedure: Divide the class into two groups. One team is in the field while the other is at bat. The pitcher shows a flashcard to the first batter. The batter has an agreed-upon amount of time in which to answer correctly (10 seconds at first). If the batter answers incorrectly, then a player in the field can attempt to answer the problem. If the field player answers correctly then the batter is out. Should the batter get the answer right, then a marker is advanced one base. Each correct answer for a batter moves him one more base until the child scores a run, at which time the next batter takes a turn. The team with the most runs wins.

SUBTRACTION

Calendar Chain. Make a paper chain containing as many loops as there are days in the current month. Use one color for the weekdays, another color for Saturdays and Sundays, and other colors for special days, such as Christmas or Valentine's Day. Use red to mark the children's birthdays that month. At the start of each day, remove the previous day's loop. Collect discarded loops into another chain to show past time. Use the chain for counting. How many days until Edgar's birthday? Which chain is shorter—past time or future time?

Treehouse

A. Equipment: A gameboard and four markers or chalkboard and chalk, cards with subtraction problems.
B. Procedure: Draw a tree with a treehouse and four ladders. Each ladder should have the same number of rungs. Place the markers at the bottom of the ladders. Shuffle the cards and place them face down in a pile. In turn, each of two or four players or teams takes a card and states the answer. If correct, the player moves a marker up one rung. The first player or team to reach the treehouse wins.

Something Is Missing

A. Equipment: Two spinners on a gameboard; answer cards, each marked with a numeral.

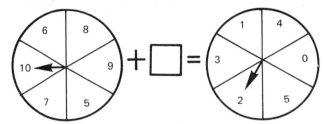

B. Procedure: The child spins both spinners and then must identify the *minuend,* the *subtrahend,* and the *product.* The correct answer card is then placed on the gameboard. If you want this game to be self-checking, write all possible problem combinations with any given minuend on the back of the answer card.
C. Variation: Move the spinners to different positions and change the sign to use the board for addition or multiplication.

Climb Up or Down the Ladder

A. Equipment: Three spinners: two with numerals, one with a plus sign and minus sign; markers, ladder gameboard.
B. Procedure: Two to six children can play. Each child begins at the bottom of the ladder. The child spins all three spinners and forms a math problem. If the problem is addition the child moves up the ladder

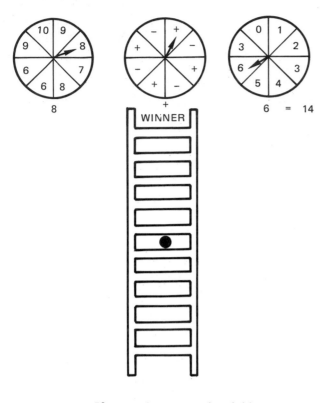

8

WINNER

6   =   14

B. Procedure: Each team starts on the 50-yard line. The first team takes a turn drawing a card and answering the problem. If the child answers correctly the team moves 10 yards forward, if incorrectly 5 yards backward. To maintain control of the ball, the team must answer three out of four questions correctly. When the first team makes two consecutive errors, the other team gains control of the ball and begins drawing cards and answering. The team with the most touchdowns in the allotted time wins.

C. Variation: Include a die marked "+" or "–." When the die reads +, the ball moves forward; – indicates backward movement. When the child responds correctly, move 10 yards forward if die is + or 5 yards backward if the die is –. If the answer is incorrect move 10 yards backward.

Puzzling Puzzles

A. Equipment: Puzzle, board on which to assemble puzzle with pieces outlined.

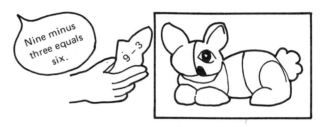

B. Procedure: Make a puzzle from a magazine picture by gluing it to cardboard and then cutting it into pieces, or use a commercially made puzzle. Mark the back of each puzzle piece with a subtraction problem. Mix the pieces in a box and let the children take turns drawing a puzzle piece. If the child gives the correct answer, he lays the piece in place. Play continues until the puzzle is complete.

C. Variation: Divide the children into two teams, each with its own puzzle, and race to see which team finishes its puzzle first.

two rungs. If it is subtraction, the child moves one rung down. If the child gives an incorrect answer, he moves two rungs down. The winner is the one who gets all the way to the top. Give an example of the marker movement before the game starts.

Football

A. Equipment: Markers, football gameboard, a deck of cards, each of which has a subtraction problem on it.

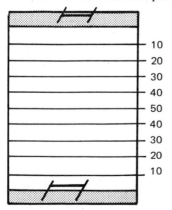

- 10
- 20
- 30
- 40
- 50
- 40
- 30
- 20
- 10

SUMMARY

It is important to provide young elementary students with many and varied opportunities to be *actively* involved in learning mathematical skills. To assist teachers in providing these varied experiences, this unit contains activity suggestions for the skills of comparing, ordering (seriation), measurement, geometry, fractions, addition, and subtraction.

These math activities are designed to make math a creative experience for young children in the early elementary grades. They are intended only as a beginning to the many creative math experiences you and the children will design.

LEARNING ACTIVITIES

A. Design a game to teach addition. Bring your game to class and explain it to your classmates. Use the game with a small group of children. Evaluate your experience and share the results with your classmates.

B. Choose one of the subtraction activities in this unit. Use it with a small group of children. Evaluate your experience and share the results with the class.

C. Choose one of the activities for teaching classification. Use this activity as a basis for designing similar activity.

D. Design an activity based on one of the ordering activities in this unit.

E. Choose one of the games in this unit. Play it with your classmates. Based on your experience, how would you change the activity?

F. Begin a card file on games for teaching early elementary mathematics skills. On each card, include the following: skill being taught, name of game, grade level, number of players, equipment required, rules or procedures.

UNIT REVIEW

1. Describe three activities appropriate for teaching classification and ordering (seriation).
2. Describe three activities you would use to help teach early elementary students geometric concepts.
3. Describe three activities you would use in teaching fractions to early elementary students.
4. Describe three activities appropriate for teaching addition skills.
5. Describe three activities you would choose to teach subtraction skills to elementary students.
6. Describe three measurement activities that you feel would be appropriate for elementary students.
7. Describe three activities you would use to teach the mathematical skill of comparison to early elementary students.

ADDITIONAL READINGS

Maxim, George W. *Learning Centers for Young Children.* New York: Hart, 1977.

Richardson, Lloyd I.; Goodman, Kathy L.; Hartman, Nancy N.; and LePique, Henri C. *A Mathematics Activity Curriculum for Early Childhood and Special Education.* New York: Macmillan, 1980.

Reys, Robert E., and Post, Thomas R. *The Mathematics Laboratory.* Boston: Prindle, Weber and Schmidt, 1973.

Unit 6 Special Topics in Mathematics

OBJECTIVES

After studying this unit, you will be able to

- describe how children's books can be used to teach skills in the early elementary mathematics program.
- describe how math skills can be reinforced through movement activities.
- give at least three examples of movement activities that reinforce math skills for children in the early elementary grades.

As we learned in Unit 5, young children in the early elementary grades learn math skills in many ways and places. In this unit we will see how math experiences can be planned using (1) children's books and (2) movement activities.

MATH AND CHILDREN'S BOOKS

Children's books are another resource for math activities. In the following teacher's report, learning about animals from children's books was the beginning of a whole lesson on shapes and colors, as well as skill in matching.

Teacher's Report 1

Learning about animal homes and telling the difference between shapes and colors were natural outgrowths of reading *Swimmy* and *Fish Is Fish,* both by Leo Lionni (both Pantheon). *Swimmy* is a story of a tiny red fish who organizes other small fish into a large school in order to frighten away dangerous fish. The story *Fish Is Fish* tells about the friendship of a frog and a fish. Both suffer from a bad case of thinking the grass is greener on the other side of the fence until they realize how well suited they are for their own environments.

To help the children identify three basic animal homes I collected pictures of air, sea and land animals. I labeled three large sheets of tagboard with *land, sea* and *air* and pasted on an illustration of a representative scene. I then asked the children to match the pictures to the animal homes.

I reinforced my students' skill in recognizing shapes and colors with a fishing game. To begin, I made "boats" by using banana split dishes or sundae containers. For a make-believe rudder and the identifying marker for each boat, I cut out and pasted one shape (such as a red circle, blue triangle or green square) at the end of each container. Then I cut out corresponding shapes from construction paper and attached one paper clip to each shape. I made fishing poles by gluing one end of a 6" piece of string to a small magnet and the other end to a popsicle stick.

I put the "tackle" on a table, placed the boats in one corner, the shapes in the other, and had the students "go fishing." I explained that the object of the activity was for them to use the magnet to pick up the paper-clipped shapes and put them into the boats with the matching rudders. (Anderson, 1981).

In the report that follows, another teacher used a book about a caterpillar to initiate practice with math skills.

Teacher's Report 2

The critter in *The Very Hungry Caterpillar* by Eric Carle (Philomel Books) eats one apple on Monday, two pears on Tuesday, three plums on Wednesday and so on until Sunday, when he eats one big green leaf. In no time at all the caterpillar turns into a beautiful butterfly.

I was getting tired of my day-of-the-week train calendar, and so were the children. Instead of representing each day with a train car, I decided to take a "leaf" from this book and use food for the days. The result—a unique weekly calendar—reinforced the children's number and color concepts and introduced the idea of metamorphosis.

On seven sheets of paper, I drew the shapes of the fruit that the caterpillar ate on each particular day of the week. Under each drawing I wrote the number of items the caterpillar ate and the day. Then I posted the sheets in their correct sequence on the bulletin board. Before long the children could identify each day by looking at the display. For example, they would say, "Today is the day the caterpillar ate three plums, so it must be Wednesday." (Anderson, 1981)

These are but two examples of many popular children's books that can help you plan math activities in interesting ways. By using books that capitalize on children's natural interests and enthusiasm, you can weave math skills into the classroom in many areas.

USING MOVEMENT ACTIVITIES TO TEACH MATH

Over the centuries literature reveals that physical activity has often been associated with intellectual development. Plato stated, "In teaching young children, train them by a kind of game, and you will be able to see more clearly the natural bent of each."

Math skills can be taught through movement activities like games and other large motor play. Using active games to teach basic math concepts reaches the three major areas of a young child's learning: (1) cognitive learning (intellectual); (2) affective learning (feelings and emotions); and (3) psychomotor learning (physical). Games reach the child's affective level through the fun and positive attitudes associated with games. Games reach the cognitive (intellectual) level by including math

FIGURE 6–1 Cooking activities provide a total learning experience: (1) cognitive learning in math (measurement); (2) affective learning (feelings); (3) physical learning (hand–eye coordination in pouring, mixing, and stirring).

skills in the games. Psychomotor (physical) learning goes on throughout as children use their large and small muscles.

For example, a child can practice math skills as well as physical skills if given task cards like the following.

```
Can you jog in place:
      8 - 1 = ____
times?
```

```
Try jogging
    10 - 4 + 2 + 3 = ____
times.
```

Using movement activities like this can help young children grow in math skills in a *total* way—physically, intellectually, and emotionally. Following are additional movement activities for math practice.

Measurement
How Big Am I?
A. Equipment: Boxes, cartons, tables, chairs, barrels, unit blocks, building blocks, play tunnel.
B. Procedure: Challenge the children with questions like the following.

- Can you build a building with blocks as high as you are tall?
- Can you build something as high as your arm is long? as high as the top of your leg? waist? shoulder?
- Can you line yourselves up with the smallest child in the front and the tallest child in the back?

C. Variations: Put two tables or chairs about the width of a child apart. Have the children go between them without touching.

Set up two or three objects of varying heights in a row and have the children go under.

Shape Identification Game
A. Equipment: Various shapes.
B. Procedure: Children are in scatter formation. When the teacher holds up a triangle, they can only move their heads. When the teacher holds up a circle, they move only legs. For a square, they move only shoulders. For a rectangle, only hips. For an oval,

they move their entire bodies. Change shapes rapidly. If you have the "Movin" record by Hap Palmer, use this record and sing "Funky Penguin." The music makes it more enjoyable for the children.

Geometric Shape Crawl
A. Equipment: Geometric shapes made out of cardboard or wood (hula hoops may be used).
B. Procedure: Spread the shapes around a space. Challenge the children to crawl through the shapes with questions like:

- Can you crawl through without touching the sides?
- Can you crawl through using one arm and both feet?
- Can you crawl through using one foot and both hands?
- Can you crawl through with one arm and one leg?
- Can you crawl through on your back using arms and legs?
- Can you put half your body through and return?
- Can you put one arm and one leg through and return?

Shape Matching Game
A. Equipment: Five or six colors of construction paper cut into shapes (circles, squares, triangles), one piece per child.
B. Procedure: The children are seated in a circle. Each child places her marker in front of her. The teacher calls out one of the shapes, at which time all having that shape run around the circle in the same direction and back to their places. The first one seated upright and motionless is declared the winner. Different kinds of movements can be specified (skipping, galloping, walking, hopping, etc.).
C. Variations: Use colors instead of shapes. Make your color and shape cards into necklaces.

Numbers
Flash Cards
A. Equipment: Flash cards (large enough to see from a distance) with numbers on them, or an addition or subtraction problem on each, enough for every child.
B. Procedure: The children are seated in a circle. Each places her flash card in front of her. The teacher calls out one of the numbers, and all having that number

(or a problem to which the answer is that number) run around the circle in the same direction and back to their place. The first one seated upright and motionless is declared the winner. Different kinds of movements can be specified: skipping, galloping, walking, hopping, etc. After a period of play, leave the markers on the floor and move one seat to the left.

Hoop Pattern With Ball Bouncing

A. Equipment: Ten hoops, two balls, two sets of number cards (1–5) placed in the hoops.

B. Procedure: Divide children into two groups of four children each. The child holds a ball, jumps into each hoop, and bounces and catches the ball the directed number of times. The first team to be completely sitting down when finished wins.

C. Variation: As children learn simple problems, cards with addition and subtraction problems may be placed in each hoop:

Counting. Review the fingerplay "Where is Thumbkin?" before reciting these rhymes and setting tasks for the children.

I can count to number one
When I count just my left thumb.
(Do one big jump)

With thumb and pointer,
That makes two.
(Do two jumping jacks)

To make it three,
Tallman will do.
(Do three toe touches)

To get to four,
I'll need one more.
So count the ringman
One, two, three, four.
(Do four body bends—front, right, back, left)

The smallest finger,
Pinkie by name,
Will make it five
To play this game.
(Do five body twists—to the right and left)

My other hand will help me, too,
To get to ten,
I'll start anew.
My right-hand thumb
Takes me to six.
(Do six windmills)

Pointer makes seven
There are no tricks.
(Do seven hops on one foot)

Then count the tallman—
That makes eight.
(Skip in small circle and count to eight)

Ringman makes nine.
No need to wait.
(Jump up and down nine times)

To count the pinkie,
Now there are ten,
And I am ready to count again.
(Run in place ten times)

Number (or Letter) Jump

A. Equipment: Grid marked off in 36 1' × 1' squares; numbers or letters.

B. Procedure: Give the sequence of numbers (or letters) to be jumped slowly and clearly. Then wait 30 seconds before telling the children, "Jump." For example:

- Jump to 3, 8, 4.
- Jump to 1, 6, 9, 0.
- Jump to 9, 3, 6, 1, 5.

2	0	9	6	4	1
6	7	5	0	3	2
3	1	8	5	7	8
4	6	5	9	4	3
5	1	0	2	7	6
7	9	8	6	0	4

- Jump to B, D, F.
- Jump to M, V, W, N.
- Jump to V, W, P, D, N.

Bb	Cc	Dd	Jj	Ll	Ee
Ii	Aa	Qq	Rr	Ss	Pp
Nn	Vv	Ee	Ff	Tt	Mm
Gg	Uu	Kk	Ii	Zz	Hh
Ss	Tt	Ww	Yy	Oo	Rr
Oo	Ll	Mm	Bb	Xx	Uu

Awareness of Space

Back to Back

A. Procedure: Arrange the children in partner formation. When each child has a partner, call out the name of a body part; for example, "back to back." The first two children who touch their backs together win. Body parts which are easier to touch together should be called initially–hands, toes, knees, back, head. Parts which are more difficult to touch together –wrists, heels–may be called later.

B. Variations:

1. Groups of three or four children may touch parts together.
2. Have the children play this game in different positions, such as sitting, standing, or lying down. Specify the position and body part to be touched: "Partners will touch the back of their heads while sitting with legs crossed."
3. Combinations of body parts may also be called: "Partners touch heads and hands." Surface planes (back, side, and front) may be used to further challenge the partners.
4. Let the children suggest combinations.

Poison Ivy. Define a small area in which the children may move. Ask the children to move around in this space without touching anyone with any part of their bodies. If they do touch someone, they will get "poison ivy" and must sit down on the side until it heals. Call out instructions for the children to change direction, pace, and type of movement.

Building Blocks

A. Equipment: Large building blocks of wood or plastic (one for each student).

B. Procedure: Each child has a block. Ask questions like:

- How many different ways can you find to get around the block?
- Find a way to get over the block.
- Can you find other ways to get over the block?
- Can you get over the block using just two parts of your body? Try three parts of your body.
- Find a way to get onto the block and then fly off into space.
- Find other ways to get onto the block and fly off in a different way. Use as many different parts of your body as possible. Have you tried using different levels and different directions?
- Can you balance on one foot on your block?
- What other parts of your body can you balance on?
- Get on your block and make a skinny shape at a low level.
- Make as many shapes as you can think of while on your block.

Make an obstacle course and let students find different ways to get through the course.

Balloon Fun

A. Equipment: One balloon per child (or use Nerf balls).

B. Procedure: Be sure the children are spaced evenly in the general space. Then issue challenges like the following:

- Can you tap your balloon and keep it up in the air?
- Can you hit your balloon up with your head?
- Can you hit your balloon up by using another body part?
- Can you tap your balloon up with your foot?
- Can you tap your balloon up, turn around, and then catch it?
- Can you tap your balloon up and clap five times before it comes down?
- How long can you tap your balloon and keep it in the air?
- Get a partner and put one balloon away. Tap your balloon to your friend by using your shoulder.

Show Me. This is a lesson on spatial orientation. The children should be in a scatter formation with adequate room between each child. Issue challenges like the following:

- Show me how small you can be (also how tall, wide, tall and thin, long and thin).
- Point to the farthest wall; touch it and return to your own place.
- Point to the nearest wall; touch it and return to your own place.
- Standing in your own place, make your feet move fast; slowly.
- Move your hands fast; slowly.
- Show me how slowly you can walk.
- Show me how fast you can walk.
- Be a tree; wall; ball; river.

Guide the children toward looking at objects in the room and noticing where they are located. Have the children close their eyes and then point to objects in the room that you call out; for example, the door, flag, chalkboard, window, wastebasket, floor, ceiling, playhouse area, wagons, play toys, hoops, teacher's desk, outside play area.

Mathematics Concept Words
Shadow Designs

A. Equipment: Opaque projector, movie projector, or other light source.
B. Procedure: Aim the light from the projector against a wall, and have a child step in front of the light creating shadows. Give directions like:

- Make your shadow as big as you can.
- Make it as small as you can.
- How tall can you make your shadow?
- How short can you make it?
- Can you make your shadow very wide?
- Pretend you are a bird. Can you make your shadow look like a bird? (Use animals also.)
- Move only your fingers. Keep watching your shadow as you move them in many ways.

- How many different ways can you make your arms bend? What part of your arm bends? (elbow) Can you make your arms bend at the elbow and then stretch them out again? Watch your shadow as you move. Do the same, but with your legs (bend at the knee), head (bend at the neck), feet (bend at the ankle), hands (bend at the wrist), body (bend at the hips).
- Can you make a design with your shadow? What else can you make your shadow do? Can it jump up? Can it hop? Can it walk? Can it run in place? Can it leap? Can it skip?
- Can you think of anything else your shadow can do?

Levels and Size. Let the children experience moving at high, medium, and low levels. Be sure they understand the concepts. Mix the levels and have them change more quickly. Have the children think of animals to demonstrate different levels: giraffe, frog, snake, monkey, seal. Ask:

- How long can you make yourself?
- Can you change positions and still be low?
- How flat can you make yourself?
- Can you stand without looking tall?
- Can you move on this level?
- Can you think of another position?
- Can you stand on your tiptoes and reach to touch the sky?
- Which level would jumping be? Try it.
- Can you jump high and land low?
- Can you move slowly and smoothly from high to low? from low to high? from middle to high?

SUMMARY

Children's books provide ideas for teaching math skills. Using movement activities to practice math skills provides a total learning experience, since these activities involve children's physical (psychomotor), emotional (affective), and intellectual (cognitive) growth.

LEARNING ACTIVITIES

A. Choose a movement activity from the unit and use it with a group of children. Share your results with the class. Discuss how you would revise the activity so that you could use it with an older or younger group of children.

B. Assemble some movement equipment as discussed in Unit 16 of *Creative Activities for Young Children, Third Edition.* Then make up a game using the equipment that reinforces a specific math skill.

C. Choose one of the movement activities from this unit. Change it so that it becomes a new activity. Then do the activity with a small group of children. Share with the class the results of this experience.

D. As a class, choose one of the games in this unit. Play it together. Evaluate your experience. Discuss how you might change the activity for various ages of children.

E. Choose at least two children's books that you could use to reinforce young children's mathematical skills. Explain how you would plan to use them. If possible, use them with a group of children and discuss your results.

F. Make a card file on children's books that teach about numbers. Be sure to indicate grade level and the specific skill the book addresses.

G. From a school supply catalog, choose some movement equipment that you would use to teach math skills. Explain your choices.

ACTIVITIES FOR CHILDREN

Shoot the Basket

A. Equipment: Use four basketball goals if they are available to you. If not, two basketball goals will be sufficient. Team A and B can challenge Team C and Team D. Use flash cards with number problems; for example:

| 2 X 5 | | 7 + 3 | | 2 − 1 |

B. Procedure:
1. One member of Team A holds up a flash card so that one child from both Teams C and D can see the card.
2. The two children try to give the answer to the problem. If they are correct, they score one point for their team and are eligible to shoot one basket (which, if made, scores one more point).

C. Variations:
1. Children may attempt to get a basket the same number of times as the answer of the problem. If the answer is correct, one point is scored, then one point for each successful basket.
2. Use spelling or vocabulary words in place of number problems. A member of the opposite team calls out spelling words. Players must spell the word correctly to earn a point and may then attempt a basket.

Blackboard Relay

A. Divide the class into three or four teams, each lined up one behind the other.

B. The first child in each line writes a number on the board and then goes to the back of the line. The next child writes a number under the first one, and so on.

C. The child who was at the end of the line should be the one to add all the numbers together.

Bean Bag Toss

A. Equipment: A cardboard gameboard, with holes cut out in different geometric shapes, that can be propped up against a wall.

B. Procedure: Points are scored for throwing bean bags through the various shapes. The child must add up her own points. The child with the most points is the winner.

C. Follow-up activities:
1. Make a collage of geometrical shapes.
2. Make a picture of a person composed entirely of geometric shapes.
3. Make shapes using toothpicks.

Geometric Relay

A. Equipment: Provide five large tagboard shapes and five small tagboard shapes. There should be enough small shapes for each child to have one.

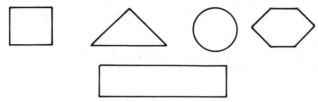

B. Procedure: Divide the class into two teams and give each child a small tagboard shape. Place the large shapes 30 to 40 feet in front of each team. On the signal, have the children who are first on each team run to the large patterns and place the smaller one on top of the matching large figure. The first squad to do this correctly and return to its original position wins.

C. Variations: Children can run, hop, or skip around their individual shapes.

UNIT REVIEW

1. Describe how children's books can be used in the early elementary mathematics program to teach skills. Give two examples in your reply.
2. What three major areas of a child's learning are involved in movement activities? Give examples of how these are involved in games.
3. Give at least three examples of movement activities that can be used to reinforce math skills.

ADDITIONAL READINGS

Anderson, Jeannette A. "Ten Tales: Books with a Bonus." *Teacher.* January, 1981.

Hirsch, Elisabeth S. "Block Building—Practical Considerations for the Classroom Teacher." In Hirsch, E.S. (ed.), *The Block Book.* Washington, D.C.: National Association for the Education of Young Children, 1977.

Johnson, Harriet. *The Art of Block Building.* New York: John Wiley, 1977.

Moursund, David G., and Shutt, Douglas L. *Calculators in the Classroom.* New York: John Wiley, 1981.

Nichols, Eugene D., and Behr, Merlyn J. *Elementary School Mathematics and How to Teach It.* New York: Holt, Rinehart and Winston, 1982.

Paige, Donald D.; Thiessen, Diane; and Wild, Margaret. *Elementary Mathematical Methods,* 2nd Ed. New York: John Wiley, 1982.

Richardson, Lloyd I.; Goodman, Kathy L.; Hartman, Nancy; and LePique, Henri C. *A Mathematics Activity Curriculum for Early Childhood and Special Education.* New York: Macmillan, 1980.

Silverman, Helene and Sheila. *Your Days Are Numbered in Calendar Math.* New Rochelle, N.Y.: Cuisenaire Co. of America, 1981.

Unit 7 Social Studies: Understanding Self

OBJECTIVES

After studying this unit, you will be able to

- discuss how children gain basic understandings about families.
- describe at least three activities to develop the concept of families.
- describe at least three activities to develop the concept of homes.
- discuss how children learn about neighborhood and community.
- describe at least three activities to use when teaching about the neighborhood and community.

In the early elementary grades, young children are expected to learn many things about being part of a group, as well as about themselves and others. In being with other children and adults in school, they learn how to get along with people outside the family and how to express emotions in a socially acceptable way, and they learn more about themselves as distinct individuals. They also learn to appreciate, accept, and appropriately express the fact that other people are different from themselves. Our discussion of social studies in the primary grades is divided into two units: Understanding Self and Understanding Others.

DEVELOPING AN UNDERSTANDING OF SELF

The development of self-concept is part of a child's total development. The child's self-concept is directly related to the way he is treated, the way he is valued by people in his life.

In the early elementary years, children are at different levels in social development, just as they are in physical and intellectual development. Some children, for instance, may have brothers or sisters and be well on the way to learning how to share an adult's attention. Others may be only children living with an adult's undivided attention.

Despite these differences, there are many common social expectations held for all young children in general.

For example, as members of a social group, all young children are expected to eventually feed themselves and to use some form of language to express their needs. Another expectation made of young children is that they know about themselves in a social sense.

FIGURE 7-1 Learning to share is part of learning to be a true member of the group. Adults help children by encouraging them to take their proper turns in classroom activities.

A.

B.

C.

D.

FIGURE 7–2 Encourage children to discuss the makeup of their own special family. Here the child drew a picture of each family member even though her parents were divorced and lived in different states. She even included her cat, which lived with her father 500 miles away.

Where Do I Belong?   Learning about one's self, family, community, and place in them are basic social learnings that take place in the early elementary years. In daily interactions between children and adults, these ideas develop gradually and naturally, as children learn to answer the question, "Where do I belong?"

Families.   In contact with others, a child learns that each person is a member of a different, separate family, and that families differ in size and composition from his own.   The child also learns that families may change in size and location over time.

Two basic ideas about families that are most often emphasized in the early elementary grades are: (1) the definition of a family in terms of relationships and, (2) ways in which families change.   The following activities may prove helpful.

Suggested Activities: Families

- Ask, "Who lives with you in your house?" Help the children understand that we usually think of a family as those people who live in the same house.
- As the teacher points to different pupils, have the children try to recall the specific family compositions of their classmates.   Generalize about what constitutes a family: Do families have to be any special size? Do there have to be both children and adults in a family? Do all families have identical members?
- Children may make individual or class scrapbooks by cutting and pasting pictures from magazines to illustrate their families.   Suggest that they compare their families' composition and size.
- Children construct puppets from popsicle sticks, paper, and crayons, and anchor them in clay.   There should be a puppet for each family member.   These may be displayed for discussion or used in dramatic play.
- Discuss the idea of multiple relationships.   For example, the child's mother is also the daughter of the grandmother.   They are children of their parents as well as grandchildren of their grandparents.   Invite a family to the class.   The child and each family member introduces the others as they are related to him.
- Discuss ways family members can change over time.   For example, the body changes by growing; the children can do things now that they could not do when

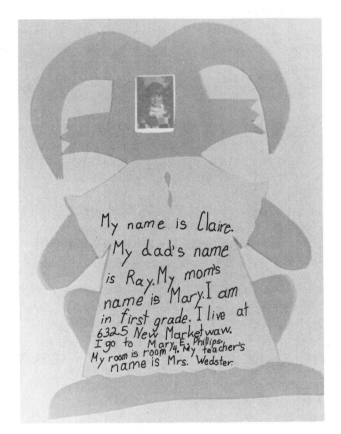

FIGURE 7–3 Writing about one's family is a good activity for the beginning of the year.

they were younger.   Their place in the family may change due to a birth, marriage, or death of a family member.   Children may bring and compare photographs of themselves and their parents and grandparents as children and at present.   Note the changes that have taken place in size, hair color, skin texture, and dress.
- Ask for volunteers to play roles of mother, father, sister, brother, etc.   Encourage children to play such roles as teenager, brother in the army, five-year-old, and baby.   The children may decide to grow up and marry or leave home.   A new baby may arrive.   Have the children count the family members each time one leaves home or arrives or a baby is born.   Those leaving home might establish a new home somewhere in the room and may want to choose someone in the class to marry.

- Take advantage of opportunities which may arise in the classroom to help children better understand death. If a pet dies, be sure the reason is understood. A good story also helps: *My Turtle Died Today* or *The Dead Bird* (Margaret Wise Brown).
- Discuss the jobs different family members do.
- Encourage the children to play family roles in the housekeeping center and block corners—cooking, cleaning, washing, ironing, caring for baby.
- Talk about ways families have fun together: play together, travel together, go to church together, sing together, go shopping together, eat together, work together.
- Read stories dealing with parents' occupations. Then have as many fathers and mothers as possible come to class and tell the children about their work. Visit as many places of business as possible, pointing out each worker's contribution to society.
- Use pictures showing various role models and discuss: What do babies do? What do mothers do? What do grandparents do?
- Talk about family pets. You may have a classroom pet show.

Suggested Activities: Homes. The fact that families live in different kinds of homes is another way to develop the idea of family likenesses and differences.

- Show a picture of a house. Ask: "Why do you live in a house?" "Does everybody live in a house?" "What does a bird use a house for?" "Does it keep him warm or keep out the rain?" "What does keep the bird warm?" "What does a rabbit's house look like?" "What keeps a rabbit warm?" "What does a turtle use for a house?" "What protects the turtle?" Have pictures of various kinds of houses, such as a nest, barn, apartment house, motel, tent, trailer, doghouse. Hold pictures up and let the children name them and tell who lives there.
- Tell the children to think of as many kinds of homes as they can for you to write down to see what a long list they can make.
- Discuss with the children how they all live in different kinds of houses, that their houses are of different colors and materials; for example, wood, brick, and stone. Have on a table a brick, a piece of wood, and

a stone. Have children feel them, tell where they came from, find heaviest, lightest, smoothest, softest, etc. Ask, "What kind of houses did people build before there were any stores, factories, or machines?" Tell the children to look at the color of their houses and to see and feel what material they are made of.

- Dramatize this song, sung to the tune of "Mulberry Bush":
This is the way we chop the trees. . .
This is the way we saw the wood. . .
This is the way we hammer the nails. . .
And so on.
- Have children draw pictures of their homes. Include color, correct number of stories, windows, doors, porches, decks, and so on.
- Show pictures of other types of houses and discuss them: Eskimos (ice houses), swamp dwellers (houses on stilts), city people (tall houses), the president (White House), a king (castle), beach houses on pilings.
- Display pictures of homes under construction, including pictures of plumbers, electricians, crane operators, carpenters, painters, and brick masons. Ask, "What tools are the workers using?" "What machines?" "What materials?" "What kind of clothes are they wearing?" "Why?" "What do they use nails and cement for?" "Why do they paint some buildings?" "Do the same workers do every part of the job?" "What do we call the people who do these special jobs?" Show a blueprint also and let the children examine it.

Neighborhood and Community. Children first learn about community through their own neighborhoods. When a child is old enough to venture out alone or with others from his own home space into other play areas, he naturally experiences his world on a larger scale. In a normal everyday way, the young child sees where others live, what kinds of houses they live in, different kinds of buildings, schools, and stores. Usually by the time he enters kindergarten, a child has a basic understanding that the other places in and around his home are his neighborhood.

At the kindergarten level and above, teachers often build on the young child's basic knowledge of neighborhood by applying the concept to the classroom "neighborhood" and its place in relation to other rooms and then to the school building itself. Map activities can involve this first school neighborhood, as in the following.

Suggested Activities: Maps of the School
- *First Maps:* Spread a large piece of kraft paper on the floor. Explain to the children that they are going to make a picture of their room. Have the children take off their shoes. Have one child at a time stand on the paper. Ask: "What do you see on this side of the room?" (Don't use words like north, south, left, or right.) When the child names an object, have the child draw it and the teacher label it on the kraft paper. Repeat the experience outdoors in the playground, too.
- *Street Maps:* Hang two or three street maps of the areas where the children live at their eye level in the room. Have the children attach construction paper or fabric flags with their names written on them to show the location of their homes on the maps.
- *Map a Dream:* After the children have had some experience with maps of real places, ask them to draw maps of their dream places. Where would they like to live? Near the sea? Near the mountains? A city? An island?

Mapmaking should be kept very simple because it is quite an abstract activity. Adults need to understand this and not expect too much accuracy in scale or details.

Suggested Activities: Neighborhood Walks. A natural follow-up activity at all levels (preschool–grade 3) to building a block model or making a map of the neighborhood is to take a walk through the school neighborhood.

- Point out where children in the class or known members of the school live.

- Develop awareness of street signs, house numbers, fire hydrants, mail boxes, traffic, various house styles and building materials, trees and other vegetation, birds, and weather conditions. The possibilities are limitless.
- If possible, arrange to visit one of the children's homes. The child can explain what various rooms are used for. The child's parent might be willing to tell the children how he keeps house, showing them some of the utensils and equipment he uses.
- Extend the children's knowledge about various kinds of homes by visiting a duplex, apartment house, or house trailer.
- Through discussion, help the children understand that there are many ways to live rather than one best one. Discuss how the needs of individuals are met through various living accommodations. For example, a big family needs a big house, an older couple needs a small house. Some people live in trailers because they like to live in different places and they can take their house with them. People who live in apartments don't have lawns to play on, but they also don't have to mow the grass.

These ideas are best brought out in informal talks. Long, formal discussions with this age group don't work.

SUMMARY

In the early childhood years, a young child learns who he is, as a separate individual and in relationship to others. Adults play a very important role in a young child's social development, by positively accepting the child as she is.

Social studies in the early elementary years generally deals with the child's developing sense of self, family, neighborhood, and community. Other important social studies issues are discussed in the following unit.

LEARNING ACTIVITIES

A. *Self-Study Activity:* Examining your own convictions.

1. Complete the statement, "I believe that. . .," and list evidence to support your conviction.

2. Now write a statement which is the direct opposite of your conviction. For example, if you wrote, "People are good," you would now write, "People are bad."

3. List evidence to support this point of view.
4. Now compare the two lists and reevaluate your conviction. Do you want to change your conviction to increase its validity? For example, one might change "People are good" to "People are sometimes bad and sometimes good," "People are neither bad nor good, only their behavior can be judged," or "Some people are bad, some are good."
5. In a similar fashion adults can encourage children to evaluate their beliefs in light of evidence.

B. Read the Edwards and Lewis review of literature on children's definitions of age (see Additional Readings). Discuss the difference in awareness of age from two years of age up until about seven. Also, discuss how children (like kindergarteners) view younger children (toddlers). What are the implications of this research for early childhood teaching?

C. Conduct a survey in the class, noting the size and composition of the families of each of the students. Discuss the differences and similarities found in the survey.

D. Conduct a class survey about the type of housing each student lives in. Record all the forms of housing. Discuss the similarities and differences. Would you expect the same for the children with whom you work?

ACTIVITIES FOR CHILDREN

My Favorite Things Book

A. Provide each child with duplicating masters that each have a question or a fill-in-the-blank sentence about favorite activities and people. Draw simple pictures to illustrate the topics for nonreaders. For example, "In winter I like to _____," will have more meaning for a child who doesn't read if there are sketches of a snowman, mittens, ice skates, or a sled. Other pages could read: "In summer I like to _____." "My favorite store is _____." "My favorite person is _____." "My favorite toy is _____." "I got _____ for Christmas/Chanukah."

B. Young children can complete the pages with drawings and/or dictation, while older children may enjoy writing their answers.

C. Staple the pages together and provide a title page, "My Favorite Things," on which children can write their names (they are now "authors") and add decorations.

D. Encourage them to "read" their books to themselves, other children in the class, parents, and anyone else who will listen. Make a special place in the reading area to display these original and highly personal books.

Telephone Tree

A. Trace the outline of a big tree on kraft paper and tape it to the wall.

B. Cut telephone shapes from construction paper and have each child write his name and telephone number on a cutout and tape it to the tree.

C. House shapes (apartment shapes, trailer shapes, etc.) with the children's names and addresses can also be made and taped to the tree.

Susan B. Anthony Day

A. Consider the fact that most schools close only in honor of men. Can you think of women who should be honored by holidays?

B. List all suggestions on the board.

C. Then do a bit of research into these women.

D. Design some activities to celebrate such holidays.

Going to BIG School

A. If a middle school, junior high, or high school is located nearby, there may be opportunities for the children to visit classes or activities that would be of interest to them in their learning about the community. For example, after clearing with the administrators and teachers, the children might visit:

- Band, orchestra, or chorus rehearsals.
- A play rehearsal if it is an appropriate one for the children.
- A stage set as it is in the process of being built and after it is completed.
- Physical education classes in the gym or a practice session on the athletic field.

- A hobby show, art fair, or science exhibit.

B. Watching such activities gives the children practice in crowd manners and behavior. It also gives them an opportunity to observe older children and their specialized activities and may help them develop an early interest in activities that will be open to them in later years.

C. These visits should be informal and last not longer than about fifteen minutes. Attendance at lengthy performances or athletic events is physically taxing for young children.

Personal Flag Activity (Grades K, 1, and 2)

A. The teacher begins this activity by holding up a symbol (for example, a stop sign) and asking if anyone knows what it is.

B. The teacher may then continue, "Yes, it is a stop sign. It's a popular sign that many people recognize. I have some other signs with me, too. Look at this one and see if you can tell what it means." The teacher may then hold up a dollar sign, for example, and continue, "Can you think of others?"

C. The teacher should then explain that a symbol is a picture or design that stands for something, just as the peace symbol represents the idea of peace. "People make symbols. Someone makes up the symbol and the rest of us learn what it means. Let's see if we can make up some of our own." The children can then work as a group in making up symbols for such concepts as happiness, spring, sadness, family, and sports.

D. The teacher may then show a picture of an American flag and explain that a flag is another kind of symbol and consists of many parts. "Does anyone know what the stars stand for? the stripes? the colors? Every country has a flag and the different parts of the flag stand for something that is important to the people. Today you are going to make your own *personal* flags, and make symbols for things about *you*."

E. The personal flag may be used to identify feelings toward a variety of people and situations, such as family, friends, school, community, and special moments.

F. After the children have completed their drawings the teacher can then lead a discussion in which the students are asked to share the meanings of their symbols with the rest of the class if they wish. At this point it is important for the teacher to keep in mind that it is not his task to give advice to the children, but rather to show interest and understanding and reflect on the value and meaning of their personal flags.

My Family

A. To help children understand the concept of family life, collect pictures of each child's family. Arrange to have some bulletin board space available for this activity.

1. Contact parents directly or send home notes requesting pictures of everyone in each child's family (individual or group pictures). Pictures of family members can be drawn by children who cannot get photographs.

2. Tape the pictures to a bulletin board or wall in clusters so that each child's family stands alone. After all the pictures have been put up, have a discussion about their families: the size, number of brothers and sisters, age differences, etc.

3. Discuss the special contributions each individual can make in his family. Try to convey the idea that children contribute to their family's well-being (for example, by giving older members an opportunity to feel proud of their ability to teach and care for someone younger).

4. Discuss some of the important functions of families. For example, you might ask, "Why is your family important to you?" "What would it be like if you didn't have a family?" "Did you ever miss your family when you had to stay with someone else?"

Classmobile Pictures

A. This activity is designed to help children achieve a better awareness of their school group.

B. Materials: One picture of each child and teacher in the group (Suggestion: If photographs are not available, children can draw self-portraits. The teacher should draw pictures of those children who are unable or unwilling to make their own.); hole puncher; various lengths of yarn, one for each picture; coat hanger; and rubber cement.

1. Before the group actually meets, select pictures of similar sizes and glue them together. Punch a hole in the top of each picture or picture set. (Be sure the hole is centered.) Insert a single piece of yarn in this hole and tie securely. Also, hang the coat hanger from the ceiling where the group will meet.
2. Call the children together and briefly discuss the idea that they all belong to the same group. Tell them that you would like them to help you make a mobile to hang in the classroom for everyone to see. The mobile will be made of the pictures of themselves.
3. Take out the pictures and ask the group to name those you hold up. Then take each picture (or picture set) and tie it to the hanger. When finished, encourage the children to discuss the creation. Hang the mobile at a height and location which will enable all children to make a close examination.

C. Variation: Instead of a mobile, the class can make a wall chart with the pictures.

UNIT REVIEW

1. Name two common social expectations held for young children.

2. Describe three activities that you would plan to help young children develop awareness of their neighborhood.

3. Describe three activities that would introduce elementary children to the idea of maps and how they relate to the environment.

4. Discuss some activities which you would use to introduce the idea of family, including size, differences, and similarities.

5. Describe two activities that are appropriate for teaching the concept of homes.

6. What are the two basic ideas most often emphasized about families in the early childhood years?

7. Why is a discussion about homes helpful in a discussion of families?

ADDITIONAL READINGS

Damon, William. *The Social World of the Child.* San Francisco: Jossey-Bass, 1977.

——, (ed.) *Social Cognition.* San Francisco: Jossey-Bass, 1979.

Edwards, J., and Lewis, H. "Young Children's Concepts of Social Relations: Social Functions and Social Objects." In Lewis, M., and Rosenblum, L.A. (eds.), *The Child and Its Family.* New York: Plenum, 1979.

Hirsch, Elisabeth S. "Block Building—Practical Considerations for the Classroom Teacher." In Hirsch, Elisabeth S. (ed.), *The Block Book.* Washington, D.C.: National Association for the Education of Young Children, 1977.

Kagan, Jerome. *Understanding Children: Behavior, Motives, and Thought.* New York: Harcourt Brace Jovanovich, 1971.

Samuels, Shirley C. *Enhancing Self Concept in Early Childhood.* New York: Human Sciences Press, 1979.

Smith, Charles A. *Promoting the Social Development of Young Children.* Palo Alto, Calif.: Mayfield, 1982.

Unit 8 Social Studies: Understanding Others

OBJECTIVES

After studying this unit, you will be able to

- discuss how children in the early elementary grades develop their awareness of other cultures.
- give at least two examples of activities that help children grow in their awareness of other cultures.
- discuss how to guide the early elementary child in learning how to understand her own and other's feelings.
- give at least two examples of activities that help young children express their feelings.
- discuss how children develop in their ability to be kind.

Just as important as learning to live with themselves is children's need to have good relationships with others. To do this, children need time, opportunities, and adult guidance with the complexities of social living. They need to gather information about people of all ages and in all walks of life, first hand whenever possible. As we know, children learn through family and school experiences that people are the same in many ways, yet different, too, in many ways. People are different in such basic things as taste in food, clothing, housing, and life style.

AWARENESS OF OTHER CULTURES

Part of developing an understanding of others in the elementary grades is learning about other cultures. Even the youngest child is aware that there are people in the community and the world whose looks, language, clothing, and customs differ from her own. Yet due to the young child's lack of experience and difficulty in abstracting, these ideas are not always easy to grasp.

Stereotyping should be avoided. So should lengthy explanations. Probably the best approach is to be aware of the children's limitations and to capitalize on opportunities to introduce them, to small bits of interesting information. We have accomplished our goal if, with our guidance, children learn that: (1) there are lots of

different people in the community and in the world, (2) we do things in a variety of ways, and (3) in many ways we are all alike. The following activities are suggested to reach this goal.

FIGURE 8-1 Learning about places and people very different from one's self is an important social learning in the early childhood years.

Suggested Activities: Other Cultures

- Begin with maps of the neighborhood showing where children in the class live.
- Have a large globe in the room. Make use of it to point out where a child in the room is going when she says that her family is about to take a trip; or to show where a story such as *The Story About Ping* (Flack, 1933) takes place; or to show where an aunt is stationed in the armed services. The important thing for children to understand, of course, is that the globe is a model of our world.
- Make use of appropriate literature to widen the children's horizons. (A number of suggested titles are listed at the end of this unit.)
- If a family or friend visits a different part of the country and brings back pictures, postcards, slides, or souvenirs, these might be shown and explained to the children.
- If a foreign visitor is available, she might be willing to show the children clothing or products (a few at a time) that would interest them. Foreign foods are fun to make and to sample. Foreign dances and games might be demonstrated or tried. And a few words spoken in a foreign tongue or written with different symbols can be examined and compared to the English equivalent. Of course, if there are children in the class of various ethnic groups, they can provide interesting information about their special foods and customs.
- If interest is high, try to extend it through photographs (the *National Geographic* is a good source), films of good quality, and recordings.

In discussing different cultures, the teacher should guard against such language as "Doesn't that sound (or look) funny?" Terms such as "interesting," "different," "distinctive," and "attractive" point out differences without being negative. More explicit descriptions also help avoid negative remarks. For example, saying, "Their houses are made of tree branches. They are very high," is far more enlightening than "Aren't they funny-looking houses?"

LEARNING TO UNDERSTAND FEELINGS

Youngsters in the early childhood years are just coming into touch with their own feelings. Some children

FIGURE 8-2 As children work together, they learn more about each other.

are so young they are just learning the names for these feelings and barely beginning to understand their meaning. Others are dealing with emotional changes as they make the transition from preschool to regular public school. Still others are moving from early to middle childhood and experiencing the many emotional adjustments this entails. Guiding young children in their developing understanding of their own and others' emotions is a highly sensitive, challenging part of the teacher's job. For adults are most instrumental in helping young children deal with their feelings and those of others. In order to do this, adults must be able to deal with their own feelings, too.

Consider your own emotions for a moment and your own early childhood experiences. As a child you left the security of your immediate surroundings to explore your neighborhood and you gradually left your toys behind. Later, as your relationships with those of the opposite sex began to change, you went on your first date. Remember how you felt at that special, almost frightening moment? And now many of you have left the security of your parents' home to risk a life on your own. Your future still holds inevitable change. Later, to some extent you will lose your physical strength and experience diminished sensory abilities. You may continue to grow in wisdom. And of course, you will finally face the biggest risk of all—death. Growth is change.

How do *you* feel about change? Do you look forward to the future, or do you begrudgingly hold onto the past? Do you accept or fight change? Does your view of the life cycle include both an appreciation for what has been and excitement about what might be?

Your personal approach to change has a direct affect on your relationship with young children. If you are open to change yourself, you won't shy away from their concerns about growth and development or their questions about death and aging. Your attitude toward change is conveyed in a healthy acceptance of your own life and all the changes, emotions, and challenges it brings. If you are unable to accept yourself and your feelings, you will be hampered in these areas with young children.

The following activities are designed to help young children deal with their feelings about themselves and others. You may learn about yourself by doing them along with the children (Dinkmeyer, 1982).

Suggested Activities: Learning to Understand Feelings. The following three activities are for grade 2 and up. Their objectives are to help young children identify and express their feelings. A sample unit plan is shown in Figure 8-3.

"Colors Make Me Feel" Poems. Have the children make up poems that tell how they feel about different colors. Each line of the poem can start with a different color; for example, "Red makes me feel. . . ." Children may either write down and complete the sentences or dictate their sentences for someone else to write. Poems may be written by individual children or by the group as a whole.

Variation: This can be an art activity. Have children draw pictures using shades of one color; the pictures should show how the child feels about that color.

Identifying Appropriate Feelings. Read the following sentences and ask children to choose the word that describes how they would feel.

- Your mom says, "Your papers show that you seem to be liking school." Which of these words tells how you might feel: tired, hungry, proud?

- Your friend says, "I have a good time when I play with you." (Word choices: happy, clean, thirsty)
- You are watching TV and your brother or sister changes the TV to a different program. (Word choices: cold, sick, angry)
- You discover that you've lost your lunch. (Word choices: angry, worried, hungry, sleepy)
- Your pet fish dies. (Word choices: sad, hungry, cold)

Variation: Write the word choices on the board and have the children read the words aloud and pick the one that describes the feeling.

Fill in the Missing Feelings. Read children a series of sentences and ask them to fill in the missing feeling words. To provide clues, give the initial or final sounds of the missing words. For example (Dinkmeyer, 1982):

- Carlos lost his father in a store. He was a little (worried).
- Joy and Nina are on their way to a party. They are so (excited).
- From the big grin on the baby's face, we could tell he was (happy).
- Adjana ran home to show the clay pot she had made. She was very (proud) of her work.
- When the dog chewed up his favorite book, Harold got (angry).
- Sari won two tickets to the circus. She felt (happy).

UNDERSTANDING THE FEELINGS OF OTHERS

Working with young children means reaching out to show them that you want to share something of yourself with them, and helping them to share their feelings with you and others. Teaching children is a passionate profession which challenges both your heart and mind.

Courtesy. Consider how often young children's feelings are *not* considered and how to deal with this problem. For example, how often have you been embarrassed by a well-meaning adult who says to a child, "Janey, what do you say to (your name) when she ties your shoes?" Reminding Janey, in front of others, about what she should say is thoughtless on the part of the adult. How

ACTIVITY	COMMENTS TO TEACHERS
Objective: To help the child understand more about herself by making a personal notebook.	Time Required: Approximately 30 minutes of class time to begin project. A time limit can be set for children to complete their booklets, or time can be set aside on several occasions to discuss the progress they are making. (Perhaps three or four periods of 30 to 40 minutes each.) One teacher reported working on this activity for about two weeks.
Concept: The individual is unique with regard to her behavior and feelings.	
Materials: Notebook paper, wire clamps, construction paper for notebook cover.	
Procedure: Have children start a notebook or scrapbook about themselves. The following questions could be used, one to each page.	The teacher can use this opportunity to help children gain insight into their own personalities. Children can see how each human being has varying talents and weaknesses and learn to accept themselves and others as people of worth.
— What games and sports do you like best? — What things do you like to make or collect? — What would you like to learn to do? — What are your favorite books and magazines? — What are your favorite TV or radio programs? — What kinds of movies do you like best? — What interesting places have you visited? — What places would you like to visit? — If you could make two wishes come true, what would they be? — What do you usually do after school each day? — What do you do to help around your house? — Do you take lessons of any kind after school? What kind? — How many people are in your family? Give the ages and some information about your brothers and sisters. — What would you like to do or be when you grow up? — Do you ever feel angry, frightened, shy? — What makes you happy? — What things do you do well and what things do you not do well?	The children can be encouraged to illustrate their books. For children who cannot write or read easily, each question can be illustrated. A child may be asked to draw herself on a single sheet of paper and write her name on it. This might be the introductory page in her book. Some children will need help in writing their comments or in expressing what they want to say.
Ask children to suggest any other questions that they might like to explore about themselves. Tell them to leave plenty of space after each question as they will want to add to their booklets from time to time. They will also want to make covers for their booklets. Some may want to paste a school picture, a drawing of a favorite sport or hobby, etc., on the cover.	

FIGURE 8–3 Sample unit plan: understanding feelings

much better for the adult simply to say herself, "Thank you for tying Janey's shoe."

Then later, when the two are alone, the adult can explain what the child should do next time someone does something helpful for her. In the meantime the child and adult can make a game of practicing courteous responses. But no adult can rudely tell a child to do something and expect the child to communicate courteously with the adult. Adults should practice the habit of saying "Please," "Thank you," "You're welcome," to children.

Take advantage of opportunities to teach children how to respond to introductions when visitors come. To the whole group or to individual children you might say, "Mrs. Smith, this is Mary (or these are the kindergarten children). Mary (or children), may I present Mrs. Smith." It is hoped that the adult will respond with "How do you do," and possibly some of the children will do it, too. If not, ignore it for the time being. Later, when the visitor has left, you can teach the children in a gentle manner what they should have said. Then remind them about it every now and then saying, "I wonder if we'll have any visitors today? If we do, what will you say when you're introduced?" Courtesy is best taught through example.

Kindness. Adults who work with young children can help children *begin* to understand and care about the feelings of others. Even though young children are just beginning to be able to understand the feelings of others, they are capable of responding to other's needs. The following examples demonstrate this point:

Two-year-old Martin hears his mother crying in an adjacent room. He is alarmed because she and his dad just had a heated argument over an issue he couldn't understand. Now his father has stormed out of the house, and his mother is sad and alone. After watching her for a few moments he runs to his room and returns with his teddy bear in his arms. He timidly approaches his mother and hands her his trusted friend. His mother takes the bear and gives Martin an affectionate hug.

June (five years old) is having a frustrating time tying her shoes after arriving at her kindergarten class. Sharon, another five-year-old, notices June's problem and offers her help. June accepts the offer, and after her shoes are tied, she invites

FIGURE 8–4 Learning to be kind and aware of another's feelings is an important social learning in the early elementary grades.

Sharon to play a table game with her until class begins.

In these situations both Martin and Sharon demonstrated their willingness to lend another a helping hand. Within the limits of his own perspective Martin tried to respond to his mother's distress. Sharon took the time to help a friend. Each child responded to the needs of another with an act of kindness.

Kindness is basic to all other social skills, and if caring about others is missing in early childhood programs, what hope can our children have? Kindness is basic to friendship, cooperation, and all other meaningful social skills developed in the early childhood classroom. Yet, what exactly *is* kindness?

Two characteristics we might consider in our definition of kindness are *voluntariness* and *internal reward*. If we view kindness from the perspective of the one who offers it, *voluntary behavior* is the aspect we must emphasize. If Sharon had been forced to help her friend, we probably would not consider what she did as being kind. Do we often overlook this issue when we try to show children how to care? An adult who *demands* that a child apologize to a playmate may be doing both children a disservice. The child who makes such a forced apology may learn to hide behind a mask of deceit, and the child who hears it may learn to expect such ritualistic insincerity.

On the other hand, the person who offers a kind act does it for the benefit of another rather than for herself. If someone does something for us because they are paid to do so or because they expect to be rewarded, we are not likely to consider their help an act of kindness. Martin shared his beloved teddy bear to relieve his mother's distress rather than to get a piece of candy or a pat on the head. Sharon helped because she felt responsible for easing her friend's frustration rather than because she expected some form of payment.

Even so, kindness can have favorable consequences for those who offer it. The Chinese proverb, "a bit of fragrance always clings to the hand that gives you roses," describes the indirect benefit that may accompany kindness. When his mother stopped crying Martin may have felt relieved of some of his own distress and pleased with what he had done. Sharon may also have felt proud of her ability to offer help successfully. Such personal benefit may or may not have been the primary reason these children decided to offer their help. However, when we encourage kindness in children, we can emphasize the pride that can result from kindness and the satisfaction of sharing in the other's success. We can define kindness, then, as "voluntary behavior that is carried out to benefit another without expecting external rewards" (Bar-Tal, 1976).

Kindness is made possible by belief in one's own *significance*. If children feel important and are recognized as individuals, they are more likely to reach out to people with support and assistance. If they feel insignificant and worthless, they may either attempt to manipulate or withdraw from others. Children who feel rejected may believe they have nothing to offer. Acceptance nurtures kindness.

Kindness also depends on confidence in one's own *competence*. If children believe they can influence others and have a positive effect on social events, they are more likely to offer kindness. Respect, then, provides a foundation for kindness.

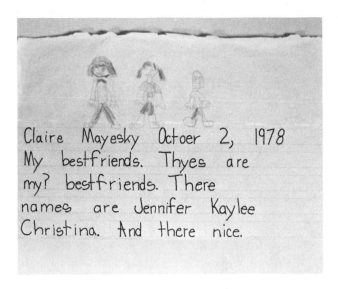

FIGURE 8–5 Best friends

We cannot help children to feel affection and to care for each other unless we first nurture a sense of significance and competence in them. When children have the opportunity to know and accept each other as distinct individuals, when they have the responsibility to make decisions, and when they feel respected by others, affection and kindness will naturally emerge in their relationships (Smith, 1982).

SUMMARY

Children can develop an understanding of others by learning about the people who live and work in their community. They can begin to develop an understanding of different cultures by a gradual introduction to different ethnic groups in their classroom and community.

The many social skills to be learned in the early elementary years, such as courtesy, kindness, appreciation of self and others, and development of ethnic and sex identity, are all introduced as much through the way adults behave and accept the children as through direct activities.

LEARNING ACTIVITIES

A. *Self-Study Activity:* The people who were kind to you.

1. Find a quiet spot where you can think without being distracted. Relax and let your mind wander back to your childhood. Try to remember someone who was significant to you, someone who took care of you and provided you with love and attention. Try to imagine this person caring for you. How do you feel?

2. Now try to remember others who nurtured you as you grew older. Maybe they were teachers, relatives, neighbors, or youth group leaders. Try to recall how each one looked and what they contributed to your life.

3. On one side of a sheet of paper list the names of these individuals in chronological order. To the right of each name describe the effect this person had on you. For example:

Mr. Holroyd, Sunday School teacher	His love for life and his interest in his students increased my own interest in others. He became the model of an educator that I wanted to become.

4. Look over this list of effects. Is there any continuity or flow from one to the other? Are there gaps in your life when no one emerged as a special person? Did others appear just at the right moment for you? If all these people were together in the same room, what might you say to them?

B. *Self-Study Activity:* messages about kindness.

1. When you were a child, what messages did you hear about kindness? What statements did your parents or caretakers make about the following issues:
   a. Generosity and sharing.
   b. Caretaking.
   c. Helping.
   d. Showing compassion.
   e. Showing affection.

2. Did their actions correspond to what they said?

3. How did their words and actions about kindness affect you?

4. Do you find yourself saying and doing these things now?

5. Are you pleased or dissatisfied with your current attitude about kindness? Can you devise a plan for change?

C. Interview an experienced first, second, or third grade teacher. Present that teacher with each of the situations below. Then ask her to answer the questions for the situation. Write their answers down and compare them. Discuss similarities and differences in their replies.

1. a. Situation: Luther ignores his fellow students most of the time. When his teacher tells the class it is time for finger painting, he grabs as many paint jars as he can. When asked to share these paints, he refuses.

   b. Question 1: In your year(s) as a teacher, have you had children who have behaved like this? Why do you think they do it? What need or needs underline their behavior?

   c. Question 2: As a general rule, what would you say is the best way to respond to this kind of behavior? Why?

   d. Question 3: What is the worst way to respond? Why?

2. a. Situation 2: Martin is a clown. If he's not making faces, he's telling jokes—and he's always disrupting the class. The other children laugh at him, but they don't seem to like him. In the schoolyard, he's generally alone.

   b. Ask the same three questions as in Situation 1.

D. 1. Ask of a six-, seven-, and eight-year-old the following questions. Record their answers.
   a. Name five children you sometimes play with.
   b. Which of these children do you like the best?
   c. What is it about them that you like so much?
   d. Of the children you named, which one do you like least?
   e. What is it about him or her that you dislike most?

2. Their answers should give you an idea of what these children think about their playmates. Discuss their statements in light of the theories of social development in Unit 8.

3. According to theories of social development, as children grow older they develop a greater awareness

KINDERGARTEN CHILD			SECOND GRADER		
	Correctly Identified	Incorrectly Identified		Correctly Identified	Incorrectly Identified
Joy Child #1 Child #2			**Joy** Child #1 Child #2		
Pain Child #1 Child #2			**Pain** Child #1 Child #2		
Surprise Child #1 Child #2			**Surprise** Child #1 Child #2		
Love Child #1 Child #2			**Love** Child #1 Child #2		
Correct answers: _____ Incorrect answers: _____			Correct answers: _____ Incorrect answers: _____		

FIGURE 8–6 Child observation form

of and interest in other children. They know more about other children; they know whom they like and why. Do the answers you received support these generalizations? Were any of the children more complete and specific in their answers?

4. Did your fellow students get the same results? Poll them and write down the totals.

E. *Child Observation:* understanding how children see other people's emotions.

1. Gather photographs or magazine illustrations that clearly show people expressing each of the following emotions: joy, pain, surprise, and love. Newspapers, especially the sports pages, may be one source of such photos. A book of photos, such as *The Family of Man,* may be another. Do not use advertisements, which present faked rather than real emotions. To keep things simple, do not select photos in which more than one emotion is expressed.

2. Show the photos to two kindergarten children and two second graders. Ask them to tell you what emotion is being expressed.

3. Indicate on the child observation form in Figure 8–6 whether each child gave accurate answers.

4. Compare your results with those of your classmates.

ACTIVITIES FOR CHILDREN

Celebrate People

Peter Spier has written and illustrated a beautiful book called *People,* which is a celebration of people everywhere. Through elaborate illustrations and a simple test, the book's large size (13″ X 10″) makes it easy to use with groups of children in any of the following activities.

A. Create a special class chart to show differences and similarities among the world's children. Include physical traits, such as hair and eyes, and cultural traits, such as clothing, family customs, foods, and religious backgrounds. Help the children contrast the pictures of Western urban life in the book with drawings of less technologically developed societies. The children will be fascinated by the pages of different pets people keep and may want to include them on the chart, too.

B. Select some of the games illustrated in the book and have your class play them. Your children may not be able to try the "Camel Rush" (from Rajasthan, India) but they could play an Afghan pulling game or "Sukatan" from the Phillipines. Many children will be delighted to hear that they already know how to play "Yobizumo," which is the Japanese word for the popular game of thumb wrestling.

Suggested Lesson Plan: Understanding Feelings

A. Lesson Goals: for each child to
   1. Find outlets for his emotions in the early childhood environment.
   2. Be considerate and conscious of other people's feelings.

B. Suggested Activities:
   1. Discuss how we all feel happy, sad, shy, disappointed, proud, lonely, angry, etc. Emphasize that it is important that we learn how to express these feelings so that we do not hurt others. Example: Have two children pretend they are playing with blocks. Ask, "How would you feel if Tommy would not let you play?" "How could you show Tommy that you were angry?" Encourage children to find an acceptable way to show feelings. Accept inappropriate expressions and help children develop more acceptable ways.
   2. Provide a wide variety of dress-up clothes and other props to give opportunity for creative role playing. During free play time children initiate their own situations for expression of feelings about self, friends, and family.
   3. Arrange the environment to display books, objects, and pictures which bring attention to emotions. Example: use media depicting attention. Ask thought-provoking questions such as, "Who do you see in the picture? How do you think they

feel about each other? Why do you think they feel that way?"
   4. The teacher may gain knowledge about individual attitudes and feelings by allowing children time to create stories. Children are thrilled to have these recorded and displayed in the room. They may also wish to illustrate various aspects of their stories.
   5. Let children listen to story records related to feelings about the dark, such as "Night's Nice" and "Who Likes the Dark?" Also *Where the Wild Things Are* by Maurice Sendak (Harper and Row, 1963) helps the children understand their feelings and fears about the dark.
   6. Encourage children to express their feelings through music. Select records with varied tempos and moods. The children express themselves through movement. Also children may finger paint to music.
   7. Make available various media with which children may work individually. Clay, painting, and hammering are good ways for children to get rid of pent-up emotions.
   8. Stimulate children to take a closer look at themselves through oral expression. Ask provocative questions such as, "How did you feel when you got up this morning? Did you want to come to school? Why did you want to come to school?"
   9. Have the children look in a mirror and make happy faces, sad, angry, surprised, scared, etc.
   10. Show pictures that express feeling: happy, sad, surprised, etc. Use different tones of voice with your back to the children, who try to guess the kind of face that would match the tone. Then the children may take turns using their voices to match the emotion in a picture.

Helping Children with Feelings of Fear

A. Monsters, the subject of many children's bad dreams or fears, undergo a new twist in *Clyde Monster,* a children's book by Robert L. Crowe (Dutton, 1976). Except for the fact that he is a real horror—a monster—Clyde is just like any other normal little boy. He has a teddy bear and his own bedroom and plays with his friends. However, he has one very unmonster-like but very human flaw; he is afraid of the dark. With his parents' support and reasoning, Clyde learns to cope with his fear.

B. To make the idea of monsters a little less scary and easier to deal with, trace a picture of Clyde on one side of a manila folder and a child on the other. On individual sheets of paper, sketch items from Clyde's monster environment and their human counterparts. For example, on one sheet show Clyde's monster night light, on another a child's. The children match the pictures to the side of the folder where they belong.

UNIT REVIEW

1. Are young children at the early elementary level capable of kindness? Explain. What are some necessary cognitive and affective skills necessary to expressing kindness? Are there different types of kindness? Explain.
2. What are the two characteristics of kindness? Give specific examples in your answer.
3. "Kindness is basic to all other social skills." Do you agree with this statement? Explain why or why not.
4. Describe two activities to help young children learn to understand their own feelings.
5. What are some ways that all children are alike, yet different? How would you help young children understand these ideas? Give examples of planned activities for this purpose.
6. What words should a teacher *not* use when discussing different countries of the world, their customs, clothing, food, etc. Why?
7. How do children learn about other cultures? Give examples of specific activities that would help children grow in their understanding of different cultures.
8. Discuss some ways to get children to express their feelings. Give specific examples of activities in your reply.
9. How do children learn to be kind? What are ways to encourage kindness in children? Give specific examples in your reply.

ADDITIONAL READINGS

Bar-Tal, D. *Prosocial Behavior: Theory and Research.* New York: John Wiley, 1976.

Dinkmeyer, Don and Don, Jr. *Developing Understanding of Self and Others, K–4* (Rev.), *Teachers Guide.* Circle Pines, Minn.: American Guidance Service, 1982.

Joyce, William W., and Alleman-Brooks, Janet E. *Teaching Social Studies in the Elementary and Middle Schools.* New York: Holt, Rinehart and Winston, 1979.

Preston, Ralph C., and Herman, Wayne L., Jr. *Teaching Social Studies in the Elementary Schools,* 5th Ed. Holt, Rinehart and Winston, 1981.

Smith, Charles A. *Promoting the Social Development of Young Children.* Palo, Alto, Calif.: Mayfield, 1982.

Books to Help Children Learn to Understand Others

Anglund, Joan E. *A Friend Is Someone Who Likes You.* New York: Harcourt Brace Jovanovich, 1958. Tells how to recognize a friend and how to be one.

Brown, Margaret Wise. *The Runaway Bunny.* New York: Harper and Row, 1972. A bunny finds he can not escape from his mother's love.

Buckley, Helen E. *Grandmother and I.* New York: Lothrop, Lee and Shephard, 1961. A small girl enjoys her grandmother's lap.

——. *The Little Boy and the Birthdays.* New York: Lothrop, Lee and Shephard, 1965. A little boy becomes so involved in giving birthday presents to others he forgets his own birthday.

Cohen, Miriam. *Will I Have a Friend?* New York: Macmillan, 1967. A kindergarten child finds a special friend in school.

De Regniers, Beatrice Schenk. *May I Bring A Friend?* New York: Atheneum, 1964. Fanciful tale about a small boy who takes a friend to tea with a king and queen.

Hoban, Russell. *Best Friends for Frances.* New York: Harper and Row, 1969. Frances is a badger who has trouble playing with her little sister and Albert down the street.

———. *The Little Brute Family.* New York: Macmillan, 1966.

———. *The Stone Doll of Sister Brute.* New York: Macmillan, 1968. Family problems are faced and solved through love and being nice.

Keats, Ezra Jack. *A Letter to Amy.* Harper and Row, 1968. Peter invites a girl to his all-boy birthday party.

———. *Peter's Chair.* Harper and Row, 1967. Peter arranges a birthday party and conquers his jealousy of his baby sister.

Lenski, Lois. *Debbie Goes to Nursery School.* Silver Springs, Md.: Walck, 1970, and *Papa Small.* Silver Springs, Md.: Walck, 1951. All of the Small and Debbie series are excellent choices for this age group.

Mannheim, Grete. *The Two Friends.* New York: Alfred A. Knopf, 1968. The first day of school is a frightening experience for Jenny until she finds a friend.

McCloskey, Robert. *Blueberries for Sal.* New York: Viking, 1948. A little girl and a little bear get their mothers mixed up on a blueberry picking escapade.

Potter, Beatrix. *The Tale of Peter Rabbit.* New York: Golden Books, 1970.

Scott, N.H. *Sam.* New York: McGraw-Hill, 1967. Everyone in this family is too busy to pay any attention to Sam. Finally someone notices his dejection and he gets a job to do.

Slobodkin, Louis. *Excuse Me—Certainly.* New York: Vanguard, 1959, and *Thank You—You're Welcome.* New York: Vanguard, 1957. Teach good manners painlessly.

Tresselt, Alvin. *Wake Up, City.* New York: Lothrop, Lee and Shephard, 1956. A description of what happens as a city wakes up.

Zolotow, Charolotte. *The Hating Book.* New York: Harper and Row, 1969.

———. *My Friend John.* New York: Harper and Row, 1968. Security is having a best friend.

Foreign Lands.

Bemelmans, Ludwig. *Madeline.* New York: Viking, 1939, and *Madeline in London,* New York: Viking, 1961. Adventures of a French girl and her fellow pupils in a Paris boarding school.

Beskow, Elsa. *Pelle's New Suit.* New York: Harper and Row, 1929. Translated from Swedish. Story of a suit from the time it is wool on a sheep to clothes on a little boy. Stresses helping one another.

Bishop, Claire Hutchet. *The Five Chinese Brothers.* New York: Coward McCann, 1938. Amusing Chinese folk tale. For five-year-olds and older.

Flack, Marjorie. *The Story About Ping.* New York: Viking, 1933. A duck lives on the Yangtze River with his uncles, aunts, and cousins.

Spier, Peter. *People.* Garden City, N.Y.: Doubleday, 1980.

Yashima, Taro. *Umbrella.* New York: Viking, 1958. A Japanese girl wants to wear her new red rubbers and carry her new umbrella, but she has to wait for rain.

Unit 9 Nutrition

OBJECTIVES

After studying this unit, you will be able to

- list the objectives of nutrition education for the early elementary grades.
- list the basic concepts of nutrition education in the early elementary grades.
- define the basic four food groups, giving at least two examples of activities to teach this concept.
- give at least three examples of activities that can be used to teach early elementary children about nutrition.

Candy and sweets have a "fun" image on TV, billboards, and in magazine advertisements. Slim, smiling, attractive people are seen munching candy bars and sipping soft drinks. Yet the effects on the human body of a diet laden with the candy bars and soft drinks are a long way from a treat.

Obviously, you can't change the nation's dietary habits. You probably can't change the meals served in the homes of the children you work with either. What you *can* do is include in the early childhood program basic information about good nutrition. Including this information is "fun" ways (as the advertisers do) will help give good health and nutrition a fighting chance in today's world of overabundance and misinformation about food and its relationship to health. For instance, in cooking activities you can introduce many important ideas about nutrition in a way that is far more interesting to children than any textbook lesson.

NUTRITION IN THE EARLY ELEMENTARY PROGRAM

Good nutrition is learned as children observe what adults will and will not eat. Children acquire a taste for either fruit or sweets as a treat, depending on where adults place the value. Will they search out candy bars and soft drinks peddled in the mass media—or enjoy nuts and raisins instead?

Children will try many kinds of foods, if adults provide the variety and model an open attitude toward new foods and food in general. An appreciation for food of different cultures is also learned by observing adults'

attitudes. It all depends on what they hear—"Ugh, I hate Chinese food," or "Chinese food sure is good!"—and on what they see—a monotonous sameness of foods, or a variety. Consider the following ways adults can affect children's eating habits:

> With most people, if you ask what their favorite foods are they'll list foods that were childhood favorites. If adults provide cookies as a reward food, then we'll think if we don't have cookies we have no self-worth.

> Better still, adults should offer non-food rewards, such as a hug. The association of food with the relief of discomfort begins in infancy. At some point in early childhood, boys and girls should be taught there are other ways to be comforted.

> Some adults used to subscribe to the theory that children's bodies tell them what they need nutritionally. That doesn't hold in our society—there's too much junk around. (Bennett, 1982)

The adult, then, is very important as a model of good nutrition for children. Little things, like having a jar of raisins and nuts on the desk instead of candy, giving a shiny apple as a reward instead of a candy bar (or better yet, giving a hug), and having frequent cooking experiences in the classroom with nutritional ingredients, are effective ways to get the good news of nutrition across to the children.

When you consider what a long-term effect you can have on children's good nutrition by setting a good example in the classroom, it shouldn't be hard to avoid having or eating junk foods and excess sweets in front of children.

STUDENT	TEACHER
Develops positive attitudes toward quality food.	Increases knowledge of nutrition.
Accepts a wide variety of nutritious foods.	Increases personal interest in nutrition and personal valuing of an adequate diet.
Appreciates the pleasurable experiences eating provides.	Increases range of teaching techniques and enthusiasm for teaching nutrition concepts.
Understands the relation of food to health and growth.	Increases inventory of teaching aides and materials for nutrition education.
Is a regular school lunch participant.	
Explores nutrition services as a future career.	Increases understanding of students, especially those in greatest need of understanding.
Is able to assist in planning, preparation, and service of simple meals.	Increases understanding of himself and others as educators.
Uses acceptable practices in handling food.	Integrates nutrition education learning activities with other subject matter.
Practices desirable habits of food selection.	

FIGURE 9-1 General objectives of nutrition education

Objectives of Nutrition Education. If you accept the challenge of teaching young children about nutrition, you assume the responsibility of providing nutrition instruction at a time in the life of each child when it will be most likely to effect changes in the child's eating practices.

Nutrition education began for each child on the first day of life and has continued each day since. This child has already built up likes and dislikes, certain habits of eating, ideas about food, and very definite feelings in regard to food at home and elsewhere.

You might conclude that young elementary students already have firmly set food habits. While this is true to some extent, your challenge will be to begin with each child at his individual stage of development and habit formation. The aspects of nutrition education that are of most concern to early elementary level teachers are:

- How children feel about food—their attitudes.
- What children know about food—their understanding.
- How children behave toward food—their habits.

These three aspects are incorporated into general objectives for nutrition education in the early elementary grades listed in Figure 9-1.

Basic Concepts of Nutrition. Implicit in the goals listed in Figure 9-1 are some concepts that are the basis of all nutrition education. These basic concepts of nutrition are:

- Nutrition is the way the body uses food. We eat food to live, to grow, to keep healthy and well, and to get energy for work and play.
- Food is made up of different nutrients needed for growth and health. Nutrients include proteins, carbohydrates, fats, minerals, and vitamins.
  - All nutrients needed by the body are available through food.
  - Many kinds and combinations of food can lead to a well-balanced diet.
  - No single food has all the nutrients needed for growth and health.
  - Most nutrients do their best work in the body when teamed with other nutrients.
  - Each nutrient has specific uses in the body.
- All persons, throughout life, have need for the same nutrients, but in varying amounts. The amounts needed are influenced by age, sex, body size, activity, state of health, and heredity.
- The way food is handled influences its nutrients, safety, quality, appearance, taste, and cost. Handling means everything that happens to food while it is being grown, processed, stored, and prepared for eating.

It is not the intent of this unit to cover each of these basic concepts. For additional information, see the resources listed at the end of this unit. In this unit, we will cover some ideas about teaching nutrition at the elementary level.

TEACHING ABOUT NUTRITION

The most fundamental nutrition concept usually taught in the early childhood years is the four basic food groups. The four types of food necessary to a balanced diet are: (1) milk and dairy products, (2) meat, fish, and poultry; (3) fruit and vegetables, and (4) bread and grains (or cereals).

Teaching about the four basic food groups not only teaches about a balanced diet, but can also help develop children's attitudes toward a life-long habit of good eating. As we know, adults must model and not just talk about good nutrition.

Teaching young children about the four food groups needn't be a one-time lesson. Just as eating occurs naturally in a child's life, you can teach about the basic food groups in the normal course of the classroom day. For example, in the following sample lesson plan, a first grade teacher used an art activity for fine motor skills (cutting and pasting) to teach about the four basic food groups. The activities in this sample lesson involved the children in learning by doing.

Sample Lesson Plan—Grades One and Two: The Four Basic Food Groups

A. Activity: Food Train
B. Equipment: Five milk cartons or shoe boxes, construction paper (red, yellow, blue, green, black), yarn, scissors, paste or masking tape, stapler, felt-tipped pens and/or crayons.
C. Procedure: Assign two or more children to cut one side or top out of a milk carton and cover the carton with construction paper. They may paste, tape, or staple the paper on the carton. The train should include boxcars, of red, green, blue, and yellow. The black engine can be decorated on both sides in any manner that the children wish. Decorate only one side of the other cars. A straw inserted through the carton on each end can serve as an axle for wheels which can be cut from cardboard or made with spools.

When the black engine and the four colorful cars have been completed, punch a hole in each end of the cars with scissors, run a small piece of yarn between the cars, and knot securely.

Label the red car "meat and fish," the green car "vegetables and fruit," the blue car "dairy products," and the yellow car "bread and cereals."

Related Activity: Classifying Foods
A. Equipment: Food models or pictures of food from magazines mounted on firm paper or cardboard.

B. Procedure: Explain to the class that the activity involves classifying a variety of foods into the color categories representing the four basic food groups. Each food model or picture should be placed in the proper car on the train.

After this activity is completed, the food models can be used for games. For example, a child may use the food models or pictures to assemble a breakfast, a dinner, a snack.

An active class game may be played by having the four food trains begin separate trips. Ask for four volunteer conductors. The conductor of each train may take in only the kind of food his train represents. For example, a child who wants to join the meat train names a meat and falls in line. Each child who falls in line must name a different member of the four basic food groups. No food may be named twice.

Cooking Experiences in the Elementary Grades. Cooking and all types of food preparation provide the early elementary teacher with many excellent opportunities to teach not only about the basic food groups, but other ideas, too. For example, in measuring and mixing a recipe, children learn many things about math—counting the number of eggs, measuring, discovering that a whole cup is made up of parts. Cooking also involves science learning about such things as liquids, powders, textures, and changes produced by mixing ingredients together. Social learning, too, is a part of cooking when children learn to wait their turns, to share in making and enjoying an edible end product together, and to appreciate individual and cultural differences in food preferences of their peers.

The following field report describes how one teacher used a cooking experience to teach several concepts:

> The making of pudding went over quite well, as do all food-oriented activities. My organization ahead of time helped it to be a pleasant and not too disorganized activity. We used instant pudding and it required a specified amount of milk to be added. This fact helped us discuss the number of cups of milk we would need, as well as the concept of milk and nutrition. They poured out the milk, measuring the amounts, and all had a chance to use the hand rotary beater to beat the pudding. This was good exercise for them all. Then we had to wait for five minutes for it to set, and this helped introduce the idea of time, and where the clock's hands would be when five minutes went by. A finger play of five monkeys was the next natural thing to do. All these things were discussed in making the pudding, so I feel that it was a true learning experience for all. However, I'm sure that children enjoyed eating the pudding at the end of the learning experience the best! (Author's log)

Nutrition concepts can also be taught with games. In the following lesson plan, the game helps reinforce concepts about the four basic food groups.

Sample Lesson Plan—Grade Two and Above

A. Group Game: Eat

B. Equipment: Paper and crayons for each student.

C. Procedure: This game can be used with a small group or the total class. Each child folds his paper so that he has a total of 16 spaces when he unfolds it (the paper is folded into quarters both lengthwise and crosswise). The columns may be colored in the order: red, green, blue, and yellow.

The child then draws 16 pictures of individual foods, one in each space. The child names each food that he has drawn and the teacher records the name of the food on a slip of paper. (This is also a task that an assistant teacher, parent, or volunteer can handle well.)

The slips of paper are mixed, one slip is drawn, and the word is read to the group. If the child has that food, he covers it with a marker as in Bingo.

"Eat" may be called when the player has covered rows horizontally, diagonally, or vertically. Or, when the child feels he has a balanced meal, he can yell "Eat" and indicate what his meal consists of. The class (or the teacher, if necessary) then evaluates the foods he has selected.

To win the game, the child may need to develop good arguments for using a variety of foods in unique and creative ways. The teacher may want to encourage these alternatives.

Children who have difficulty understanding and playing the game should have additional opportunities to repeat this activity and learn more about the four food groups.

D. Variations: For younger children, the teacher may wish the child to fold the paper twice, making only four squares. The child may color one part red, one green, one blue, and one yellow. Then as food names are called, he may put his marker down on the correct color. A child who has four sections covered may yell "Eat."

Classroom Grocery Store

A. Equipment: Orange or apple crates, with or without a large freezer or appliance box; collection of empty food containers; empty cans with labels intact; food models; cash register; play money; paper bags.

B. Procedure: Collect cans, boxes, and other food containers. Attempt to get as large a variety of foods as is practical. Include foods that may not be familiar to the children. Imported foods would offer a variety of experiences for discussion and learning.

To set up the store, place an appliance box on its side with one side cut out (or use a classroom table). Two fruit boxes should be set up vertically inside the box (or under the table), making two shelves to hold food containers.

Appoint a storekeeper and one or more assistants. Their job is to arrange the food in some logical order. For example, one day it might be arranged according to the four food groups. Another day it might be grouped according to the section of the United States or other country from which it comes; for example, corn and wheat from the Midwest; vegetables and fruit—local in season, California or Florida in winter; rice and grits—South. Labels will provide the information.

Shoppers may want to make a list before buying food at the store. These lists should include the item wanted and the food group. Encourage buying foods from each group.

Shopping in the class store might take place during a scheduled period during the day, or the children might be free to use the area whenever they have completed assigned work.

SUMMARY

Children learn as much about nutrition in daily life as in lessons. By observing adults in their lives, children learn what *not* to eat, as well as what *to* eat. The aims of nutrition education are to work with children on their attitudes about food, their understanding of the role of food, and on their food-related habits. The basic concepts of nutrition that are related to teaching early elementary level children nutrition are: (1) nutrition is the way the body uses food, (2) food is made up of different nutrients needed for growth and health, (3) all persons throughout life need nutrients, and (4) the way food is handled influences the amount of its nutrients, its safety, quality, appearance, and taste.

The four basic food groups are usually taught in the early elementary grades. Cooking activities, games, and other strategies are effective in teaching about these food groups. Nutrition information can easily be incorporated into other curriculum areas to enrich a child's exposure to these ideas.

Adults have a responsibility to monitor children's nutritional awareness in the early elementary grades. Being aware of any noticeable eating problems, relating them to parents, and following up are important aspects of monitoring children's nutritional needs. In nutrition the emphasis is placed on the establishment of good habits in the early years of life, which will make a long-term difference in the quality of life.

LEARNING ACTIVITIES

A. 1. Make some of the following snacks in class with your fellow students:

   a. Merry-go-rounds.
   You'll need:
   - Thin slices of apple.
   - Peanut butter.
   - Animal crackers.

   Spread peanut butter on apple slices. Stand animal cracker up in the peanut butter.

   b. Snack treats.
   Try raw:
   - squash
   - zucchini
   - turnips
   - green peppers
   - mushrooms
   - cauliflower

c. Pretzel sticks.
You'll need:
- Hot dogs.
- Cheese of your choice.
- Pretzel sticks.

Cook hot dog and cool. Cut cheese and hot dog into thin, bite-size chunks. Stick them on the pretzel stick.

2. Discuss what age group you would use them with and why.
3. Discuss the four basic food groups to which the foods belong.
4. Alter the snack recipes to include different ingredients from the same food groups.
5. Make up several snack recipes of your own and discuss what age group they would be most suitable for; what precautions are needed; what food groups they cover.

B. Keep a three-day record of what you eat for each meal and for in-between-meal snacks. Categorize these foods into the four basic food groups. Is your diet balanced? How would you change it to improve it?

C. Role play a group of children experiencing a type of food for the first time—perhaps eggplant, squash, or beef tongue. Have one student play the children's teacher:
1. What kinds of expressions would you make (as the children) when you taste the food?
2. How would you react when you found out what the food was?
3. Role play at least one way a teacher can act to make the children more willing to taste this new food?

4. Role play at least one to discourage children in this activity.

D. Choose one of the nutrition or cooking activities from this unit and use it with a group of children. Report on your results as follows:

1. Age of group: _____
2. Rate Lesson Success:

	Above		Below	
Good	Average	Average	Average	Poor
5	4	3	2	1

3. Explain your rating.
4. Describe the most successful part of the experience, the least successful.
5. What would you change to improve the activity?

E. List the various experiences you have observed children have with food in your work with young children. Discuss how you would improve on the experiences you observed; how you would alter them for a different age group; and how you could relate one (or several) to different areas of the curriculum.

F. Survey local community organizations, hospitals, etc., to determine what nutrition services they offer for special, mainstreamed children. Share your findings in a report to the class. If possible prepare your report with sufficient copies for your classmates. Be sure to list the special need (for example, vision impaired, crippled, etc.) as well as the particular assistance given after serving the food, and agency name, address, and contact person.

ACTIVITIES FOR CHILDREN

Nutrition Songs

Tune: "Row, Row, Row Your Boat"
Drink, drink, drink more milk,
Morning, noon, and night.
Healthier, wiser, and better you'll be,
And so increase your might.

Tune: "Mary Had a Little Lamb"
Vegetables are fun to eat,
Fun to eat, fun to eat.

For meals and snacks they are a treat,
Eat some every day.

Tune: "I've Been Workin' on the Railroad"
I've been workin' in my garden,
All the live-long day.
I've been workin' in my garden,
Cut'n grass and weeds away.
Can't you see the carrots growing,
Bigger'n and better every morn.
Can't you taste that good fresh cornbread,
Made from yellow corn.

Tune: "Home on the Range"
Oh give me a meal
From the good basic four,
I'll clean off my plate every day.
For breakfast and lunch
Or just something to munch,
Eat the 1-2-3-4 way all day.

Health, health from your food,
You can grow up much stronger each day.
For breakfast and lunch
or just something to munch,
Eat the 1-2-3-4 way all day.

Tune: "Old McDonald Had a Farm"
Old McDaniel had a farm, e-i-e-i-o!
And on that farm he had a garden, e-i-e-i-o!
There was vitamin A here
    And vitamin C there,
Fruits and vegetables everywhere,
Old McDaniel had a farm, e-i-e-i-o!

Old McDaniel had a farm, e-i-e-i-o!
And on that farm he had a cow, e-i-e-i-o!
There was sweet milk here
    And cheese there,
Strong bones and teeth everywhere,
Old McDaniel had a farm, e-i-e-i-o!

Old McDaniel had a farm, e-i-e-i-o!
And on that farm he had some hogs, e-i-e-i-o!
There was protein here, and iron there,
Rich blood and strong muscles everywhere,
Old McDaniel had a farm, e-i-e-i-o!

Tune: "Joy to the World" (pop song)
Jeremiah was a health nut,
Was a good friend of mine.
Never understood a single word he said,
But I helped him eat his bread.
Yeah! He always had some mighty fine bread.
He always had some mighty fine bread.

Chorus:
    Joy to the food!
    All the kinds of bread,
    All the fish in the deep blue sea,
    Joy to you and me!

If I was the king of the world,
Tell you what I'd do.
I'd bring out the vegetables and the milk,
And I'd cook a fine meal for you.
Yeah, I'd cook a fine meal for you.

Tune: "Skip to My Lou"
Carrots have lots of vitamin A,
To help me see when I work and play.
I eat my bread because I know.
Vitamin B will help me grow.

Orange juice has vitamin C,
I drink it 'cause it's good for me.
Vitamin D is also fine,
I get it from the bright sunshine.

When I can't play in the bright sunshine,
For my vitamin D so fine.
Vitamin pills are not for me,
When my milk's enriched with vitamin D.

Vitamins A, B, C, and D,
All are good for you and me.
They will keep me strong and well,
If I eat my food at every meal.

Tune: Coke commercial
I want to have good health each day,
I want to laugh and sing.
I want to feel and look my best
So I can "do my thing."

I need some pep to help me go,
Some strength and energy.
So every day I choose the foods,
That do these things for me.

Chorus:
    It's the real thing!
    We'll feel happy and good,
    When we choose the right food,
    It's the real thing!

Tune: "We'll Sing in the Sunshine"
Basic four I love you,
You make me strong each day.
Eating hearty menus,
The 1-2-3-4 way.

Chorus:
>We'll sing in the sunshine,
>We'll laugh every day.
>We'll sing in the sunshine,
>The fun four food group Way.

Breakfast that's a-go-go,
A zippy lunch at noon.
A sturdy meal at dinner,
We'll sing our merry tune.

Repeat Chorus

Remember to keep eating
The healthy, happy way.
And you'll sing in the morning,
And feel great all the day.

Repeat Chorus

Nutrition Activities

A. Have children draw pictures of their favorite foods and label them.

B. Collect colorful pictures of foods from magazines. Make posters, booklets, collages, or a picture dictionary of favorite and different foods from cutouts.

C. Make a food alphabet.

D. Make a bulletin board on vegetables. Give children brown construction paper with slits cut in it. Color and cut out various vegetables and put them through the slits cut in the brown paper. Add sun and raindrops to help them grow.

E. Use a fruit or vegetable grab bag using fresh foods or picture cutouts. The child identifies the food by color, shape, etc.

F. Introduce some new foods not commonly eaten by children, such as raw pineapple or turnip. Sample in class for a snack.

G. Make a food mural. Children develop a mural including a tree, grass, and sky. Then they color and cut out fruit they have drawn (or made from dittos) and hang these on the tree. Vegetables can be placed along the base of the mural (on the ground).

H. Collect pictures from magazines to illustrate the need for breakfast (girl asleep at desk, car out of gas, children fighting or crying).

I. Collect pictures of breakfast foods. Group according to those liked by class members, mothers, fathers, etc.

J. Prepare a cereal snack using a variety of cold cereals mixed with melted butter and garlic salt, toasted in oven. This will illustrate another way to serve cereal.

K. Have a snack tree. Children collect or draw pictures of snacks and attach them to a large tree made out of brown paper.

L. Cut colored construction paper in the shapes of fruit and vegetables—about the size of throw pillows. Staple two identical pieces together, leaving the top open. Children tear and crumble small pieces of newspaper and stuff the fruit and vegetables. Then they staple the top and print the name on the outside.

M. Demonstrate how to wash fruit and vegetables. Examine washed and unwashed foods under a magnifying glass. Leave bread, milk, crackers, fruit, and vegetables, unprotected for a day or two. Observe what happens.

N. Write short stories and songs about where food comes from. Describe the taste of new foods. Keep a class notebook on new foods tasted.

O. Plan a tasting party. Invite parents. Prepare placemats and decorations. Use stories and songs prepared by the students for presentation.

P. Have children make larger-than-life-size pictures of various foods to hold up before themselves. Place them on tagboard. Make a curve for the neck and shoulder ties or slits for arms. These can be used in a variety of ways. For example, dramatize: "I am milk (or milk products). I build strong bones and teeth. I furnish calcium." Play "Who Am I? What can I do for you? How am I able to help you?"

Q. Discuss food values of apples, carrots, and other crunchy vegetables as snacks. For example, they clean and strengthen teeth, while sweets are bad for teeth. Experiment: Cut an apple and a marshmallow. Which food clings to the knife? Which food clings to the teeth?

Note: See Creative Activities for Young Children, Third Edition, for recipes and more nutrition, art, and music activities.

UNIT REVIEW

1. Explain how food experiences can be integrated with other learning experiences in the curriculum. Discuss how you would plan food activities for this purpose.
2. Describe the four basic food groups.
3. Give at least two examples of activities you could use to teach about the basic food groups.
4. Describe the goals of nutrition education in the early elementary grades.
5. Describe the basic concepts of nutrition that are appropriate for the early elementary grades.

ADDITIONAL READINGS

Aronson, Aaron, and Nelson, Susan and Hannah. *Health Power: A Guide to the Health Component of Early Childhood Programs.* Philadelphia: Department of Community and Preventive Medicine, Medical College of Pennsylvania, 1981.

Austin, G.; Oliver, J.S.; and Richards, J.C. *The Parents' Medical Manual.* Englewood Cliffs, N.J.: Prentice-Hall, 1978.

Bennett, Beverly. "Children Overcome the Best of Intentions." *Chicago Sun Times,* April 21, 1982.

Boston Children's Medical Center. *Child Health Encyclopedia.* New York: Dell, 1975.

Endres, Jeannette B., and Rockwell, Robert E. *Food, Nutrition and the Young Child.* St. Louis: C.V. Mosby, 1980.

Fomon, Samuel J. *Infant Nutrition,* 2nd Ed. Philadelphia: W.B. Saunders, 1974.

Green, Martin I. *A Sigh of Relief: The First Aid Handbook for Childhood Emergencies.* New York: Bantam, 1977.

Mayesky, Mary, et al. *Creative Activities for Young Children,* 3rd Ed., Albany, N.Y.: Delmar Publishers, 1985.

McAfee, Oralie, et al. *Cooking and Eating With Children.* Washington, D.C.: Association of Childhood Education International, 1974.

Pantell, R.H.; Fries, J.; and Vickery, D. *Taking Care of Your Child: A Parents' Guide to Medical Care.* Reading, Mass.: Addison-Wesley, 1978.

U.S. Department of Health, Education, and Welfare, Office of Child Development. *A Guide for Project Directors and Health Personnel.* Day Care Series 6, DHEW Publication No. (OCD) 73-12, Washington, D.C.: Government Printing Office, 1973.

Cooking in the Classroom

Edge, Nellie. *Kids in the Kitchen.* Port Angeles, Wash.: Peninsula Publishing (P.O. Box 412, 98362), 1981.

Goodwin, Marty T., and Pollen, Gerry. *Creative Food Experiences for Children.* Washington, D.C.: Center for Science in the Public Interest (1755 S Street, N.W., 20036), 1977.

Unit 10 Field Trips

OBJECTIVES

After studying this unit, you will be able to

- explain why field trips are an important part of the early elementary curriculum.
- list guidelines for successful field trips.
- describe the pretrip preparations necessary for a successful field trip.
- list some strategies to use on the day of the field trip to ensure a successful experience.
- list positive and negative aspects of field trips.

As we begin our unit on field trips, let us see how one student teacher prepared a first grade class for a field trip—to a ballet, of all places!

Student Teaching Log Report
First Grade

February 5
This Saturday the class will take a trip to see *Billy the Kid,* a ballet performed by the Oakland Ballet Company. I am going to teach a lesson this Thursday that will prepare the class for the ballet. With the help of the school librarian I found a filmstrip and several books that were appropriate for my topic and class ability level.

February 9
Today I taught my lesson on the *Billy the Kid* ballet. I wore a cowboy hat and brought the children over to the carpet calling each of them "partner." Then we discussed cowboys and the Old West bank robbers. From our discussion, I reminded them of some things to look for in the filmstrip. The class enjoyed the film strip and was (to my surprise) quite attentive throughout. Afterward they were full of questions. Everything from "Where did all the horses come from?" to "Was this before or after the time of old cars?" I felt like the Encyclopedia Brittanica personified.

February 11
We boarded the bus complete with identification tags (so they would know where to return us if *we* got lost!). The class behaved fairly well for the duration. The comment that made my day, however, came when the music for the ballet began.

One student remarked: "Hey, this is the music we heard in school!" I was astounded that some of the students actually recognized the music after hearing it only twice two days before. *Billy the Kid* was a perfect ballet for children in that it was colorful, used familiar characters, was easy to follow, and didn't last too long. Between our discussion in the classroom and the choreographer's explanation prior to the performance, the students understood and enjoyed the ballet very much.

How many of you reading this can honestly say you have enjoyed a ballet as these first grade children did? The student teacher's planning made their enjoyment possible, as the topic of the ballet (the Old West) was taught in an age-appropriate manner. Not many of the children would easily forget a teacher wearing a western hat, acting like a cowboy! While you may not be as much of an actress as this student teacher, you *can* make field trips fun learning experiences for children.

The focus of this unit is on the enjoyable aspects of learning outside the classroom—called field trips. The unit is about organizing, preparing for, and conducting these out-of-school learning experiences. With the information provided in this unit, class trips will be more than "group escapes" from the classroom routine, and more like the following:

At the day-care center, one mother questioned her child about the class trip that day:

"There were a whole lot of old people there," four-year-old Amy noted seriously as she described her class trip to a nursing home. "Then," she added with a proud grin, "we sang for them, and after that they weren't so old anymore."

While the children were singing, faces brightened and softened. Lines of worry, depression, and pain were changed into smiles. Amy had seen the cares and burdens of age melt briefly away, and she had known the joy of helping to make it all happen.

And to Amy's teacher, all the trouble involved in arranging the visit, practicing the songs with the children, and conducting the trip suddenly seemed worthwhile.

WHY FIELD TRIPS?

Trips are a way to introduce children to the wider world around them through first-hand experiences that cannot be brought into the classroom. On trips they come in contact with new, real objects and events and with people in new and interesting roles. Trips can be used to reinforce and extend concepts already learned: colors, shapes, sizes, smells, sounds, textures, objects, events, and concepts such as those of social group and

community discussed in Units 7 and 8. Field trips can also be used to focus on certain subject areas. (See the suggested lesson plans and activities at the end of this unit.)

Trips often provide ideas for dramatic play and make pictures, stories, and songs more meaningful to young children. For example, a child who has experienced a bus trip may later enjoy pretending to be a bus driver or showing you in a picture of a bus just where the driver sits. She may take even greater pleasure after a bus trip in listening to and singing the song, "The Wheels of the Bus Go Round and Round."

Field trips need not be a single visit, but may be several visits to the same location for different purposes. For example, consider this sample activity: Find an area that you can visit regularly. Tell the children to observe everything very closely. Go back to the same area a week later. Ask the children to find as many things as possible that have changed. Is the grass taller or shorter? Are the plants growing buds or changing color? Go back

FIGURE 10–1 Field trips can be used to reinforce and extend concepts already learned, like colors, textures, smells, sounds, objects, and events in nature.

FIGURE 10–2 Field trips need not be one-shot visits, but may be several trips to the same location for different purposes; for example, to find out what has changed since the last visit.

again after several weeks. Now what has changed? On your return to the classroom, record these changes in language experience charts, in pictures, paintings, or on a tape recorder.

How to Have Successful Field Trips. There is a great deal more to a field trip than bundling a group of children into a bus and heading for the nearest zoo. Preparations for the time before, during, and after the trip are necessary to making a field trip the kind of learning experience that justifies your leaving the classroom to learn. For young children, the learning that takes place through first-hand experience on a class trip will be greatly enhanced if you follow a few general rules:

Keep the trip simple. Keep it as close to the school as possible, especially for very young children. Do not search for the exotic. Young children will probably be more excited and interested in a kitten or a rabbit that they can hold and pet than in an elephant or a museum's dinosaur that they must view from a distance.

Select a few "close-ups" for the children's particular attention on the trip and plan your learning activity around them. Although the total trip experience is of importance to the child (who may see and remember things not included in your plans), maximum learning is more apt to take place if you limit your teaching goals to a few concepts. (See the sample lesson plans at the end of this unit.) On a trip to an art museum, for instance, the large number of displays may well overwhelm and tire the children. By pointing out and talking about a special picture or two and by looking at and touching (as permitted, of course!) one or two sculptures, you will give the children something they will remember. Back in the classroom, this experience is something that can be expanded upon to develop the childrens' understanding of what art museums are all about.

Prepare the children for the trip by giving them some idea of what to expect. Pictures, stories with pictures, toy replicas, talking about what you will see and do, and describing the kind of behavior you expect of the child are all ways to prepare for a trip. Before a bus trip you might show a picture of a bus (or use a toy bus) and point out the doors and windows. Talk about how you will get on the bus at the door and will look for a window seat so that you can see all the things the bus passes on the street.

The children must be involved in planning the trip if it is to be successful. This planning must include developing the purpose for the trip; when, where, and how to make the excursion; and follow-up activities. Children in the upper grades can take more responsibility in the planning stages; elementary children need much more direction. Nonetheless, *all* children at *any* level should be involved in some of the planning.

Transportation may be necessary for some trips. A school bus usually is the preferred transportation because of insurance regulations and liability laws. If the bus tour is long, plans should be made to keep the children busy while traveling. Valuable learning may be accomplished while riding on the bus. For example, children may keep a log of their trip complete with departure time, weather conditions, road conditions, points of interest en route, and such other items as they wish to include. These can be drawings for children who cannot write easily enough to record all these details. For younger children, paper-and-pencil activities can be collected in a Busy Bag for these longer trips. To prepare a Busy Bag, collect one paper bag for each child or one bag for each pair of children (trip Buddies). The selection of items in these bags will be based on the ages of the children. The bags might include:

- A small pencil, two or three crayons.
- Recycled comics, clipped-together stories from old primers, newspaper comic sections.
- Word puzzles, word search puzzles, paper games (Tic Tac Toe, etc.).
- Shirt cardboards (heavy enough for lap boards).
- Sheets of plain paper for drawing (approximately three sheets per child of various sizes and colors).
- Prepared lists of questions, items to watch for and record on the trip (possibly for an end-of-trip prize).

Timing the trip is another consideration. Pick a day of the week when the place to be visited is not too crowded. Arrange in advance for trips that need the cooperation of others, such as guides. Plan to alternate your activity on the day of the trip with contrasting activities; quiet play or a rest period before an active trip to the park, or

General Pretrip Arrangements

_____ Letter to parents explaining trip, purpose, and other details

_____ Permission forms for parent or guardian signature

_____ Arrangements for parent volunteers

_____ Preparation of Busy Bags (for longer trips)

_____ Arrangements for nonparticipants

Pretrip Discussions

_____ Conduct rules (on *several* occasions)

_____ Things to be seen and done on trip (on *several* occasions)

_____ Stories, fingerplays, other related activities

_____ Children's plans for things to see, do, etc.

_____ What to do if you get separated from the group (role play this, if possible)

Group behavior:

_____ Staying with buddy

_____ Importance of knowing name, school name, bus number

_____ Review phone numbers, teacher's name, parents' names

With parent volunteers:

_____ Responsibilities of children, parents

_____ Rules of conduct

_____ Emergency procedures

Pretrip Site Arrangements

Contact field trip site to:

_____ Set up length of visit, date, time

_____ Set up what will be seen

_____ Set up whom to see (guides)

_____ Get any required rules and regulations for visit

_____ Get brochures, posters, and any other literature to use for pretrip discussions

_____ Get information on lunch/snack, bathroom arrangements

_____ Find out accommodations for special education students

_____ Find out admission prices (if any)

FIGURE 10-3 Checklist of preparations to make before field trips.

romping, active play before a quiet trip to the library for a story hour. A summary of these and other guidelines for pretrip preparations can be found in Figure 10-3.

Pretrip preparations at the place to be visited are essential. Several weeks prior to leaving on the field trip it is necessary to contact the people at the place to be visited to arrange guide service and make eating and bathroom arrangements and any other special arrangements for the group's visit. It is a good idea for the teacher to make a personal tour of the place to be visited to find out in advance any problems that might arise when the children visit. For example, it is important to know if a museum with a main entrance with two flights of stairs has a side entrance on ground level for groups. This is especially important for children with special needs. Restroom facilities and food services must be checked out in advance, too, to know their exact locations and capabilities for groups of various sizes.

Get parent's written consent. A parent's written consent is usually required for a child to participate in most trips away from school. If parents understand the nature and purpose of the field trip, there should be no problem in getting their permission. A sample permission letter is shown in Figure 10-4. Many schools use one blanket permission form to cover all trips taken during the year.

Read about the trip. Not only should the children discuss the upcoming trip, but some reading on the subject should also be done by both teacher and children. Reading books, pamphlets, and other kinds of information about the trip will help children know what they should look for on the trip.

Make name tags. Making name tags for a field trip is another pretrip activity that involves the children. Have students make their own brightly colored group identification tags from construction paper. These can take the form of armbands, headbands, bracelets, or even buttons as long as the children's names are boldly marked on the paper. With very small children, point out that strangers will also know their names, and remind them that they are not to go anywhere with

Dear _____

We are planning a field trip

To: _____(Location)_____

On: _____(Date)_____

From: _____(Time)_____

This trip is _____(Explanation of purpose for trip)_____

_____

If you would like your child(ren) to attend, please complete, sign, and return the form below by ____(Date)____ .

PLEASE NOTE: *You must complete and return this form in order for your child(ren) to particiapte.*

Thank you.

(Teacher's name)_____

(School phone number)_____

- -

(CUT OFF AND RETURN THIS PORTION TO SCHOOL)

Your name _____   Relationship to child _____

Child(ren)'s Name(s) _____ , has/have my permission to go on the class field trip

scheduled for _____(Date of trip)_____ .

_____   _____
Date Signed   Signature

FIGURE 10–4 Sample permission form

someone else without your permission. Assign two children to help you count heads at every change of location throughout the day.

Give some thought to the dangers that may be involved in a trip and the kinds of fears the young child may have in coping with new people and new surroundings. Make and stick to safety rules. Discuss these rules before the trip on more than one occasion. Transmit a feeling of security by holding the child's hand, putting an arm around one who seems a bit confused, and even lifting some up in crowds so that they can see what is going on.

Plan for restless times and have activities ready. For example, during a lengthy wait for the bus, one teacher introduced a hand-slapping game. Children were divided into pairs. In unison with the others, each student slapped her hands on her thighs and then slapped palms with her partner, calling the partner's name as the two slapped hands. Another teacher held a walking relay race. In this race the children formed two lines, and the players who were first in line *walked* swiftly along the outside of their own lines until they reached the back. Taking their places at the end of the line, each slapped the hands of the person in front, who turned and passed the slap forward until it reached the head of the line. This was repeated until the bus driver was ready for the class. (A class of second graders participated in these activities.)

Use the buddy system. The buddy system is another good group technique to plan on using. In the buddy system each child is assigned another child as a buddy to be with at all times. Before the trip, have several "roll calls of buddies," asking each child who her buddy is until it is obvious all children know their buddies quite well.

Get adult volunteers to help. If you are taking a group of children on a trip, keep the group as small as possible and secure the help of other adults to manage the group. With preschoolers, one adult for every two children works well. With older children, one adult for every six children is a good rule of thumb to follow. See Figure 10–5 for a day-of-the-trip checklist.

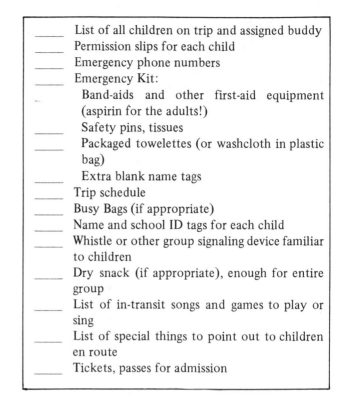

_____ List of all children on trip and assigned buddy
_____ Permission slips for each child
_____ Emergency phone numbers
_____ Emergency Kit:
_____ Band-aids and other first-aid equipment (aspirin for the adults!)
_____ Safety pins, tissues
_____ Packaged towelettes (or washcloth in plastic bag)
_____ Extra blank name tags
_____ Trip schedule
_____ Busy Bags (if appropriate)
_____ Name and school ID tags for each child
_____ Whistle or other group signaling device familiar to children
_____ Dry snack (if appropriate), enough for entire group
_____ List of in-transit songs and games to play or sing
_____ List of special things to point out to children en route
_____ Tickets, passes for admission

FIGURE 10–5 Checklist for day of field trip

Don't be overprotective of the children. Encourage trying new experiences, responding to a friendly bus driver or guide, playing with another child. These, too, are important kinds of learnings for children on a field trip.

Take the trip and enjoy it! Relax and enjoy the trip with the children. If adequate planning has been accomplished, your relaxation and that of the children will be the easiest part!

After each trip, provide follow-up activities to reinforce and deepen the learning. See Figure 10–6 for a checklist of posttrip activities. Read stories, or make them up, and look at picture books related to the trip experiences. Make a scrapbook of pictures and drawings or construct replicas of something seen on the trip. Encourage the children to act out trip experiences in dramatic play. Most important, let the children tell you or someone else all about the trip, including what they liked best and would like to do again.

Write thank-you letter from class to:
_____   Parent volunteers
_____   Site guides, bus driver, zoo manager, etc.

Note improvements needed for next trip:
_____   From children
_____   From parents
_____   Your own

Note good points to use in next trip:
_____   From children
_____   From parents
_____   Your own

Follow-up Discussion of Trip
_____   Class discussion of favorite parts, souvenirs, photos, tape recordings, etc.
_____   Stories
_____   Fingerplays
_____   Draw, paint, model favorite parts of trip
_____   Dramatic portrayal of major points of trip
_____   Class discussion of least favorite parts

Evaluation of Instructional Usefulness
_____   Did students understand the process demonstrated or gain the knowledge you had hoped?
_____   Are students able to see the connection between their trip and what you are teaching them in the classroom?

FIGURE 10–6 Checklist for field trip follow-up

FIGURE 10–7 A good follow-up activity to a field trip is to draw experiences on the trip. In this picture, a child pictures the apple trees on the farm the class visited.

FIGURE 10–8 A group mural was the result of a field trip to a farm. The teacher integrated language arts by writing each child's comments by her pictorial remembrance of the class trip.

After each trip, evaluate it. Some questions to be answered are: Was the field trip a success in the sense that it fulfilled its aim, purposes, and objectives? Was the time spent away from the classroom worthwhile, or could as much have been accomplished in the same amount of time in the classroom? How did the children feel about the trip?

Many different forms of evaluation may be used by the teacher. These may be based in part on class activities. For example, some children may wish to write and record a class story concerning their impressions, and other children may wish to draw pictures of it. Some pupils may wish to design a bulletin board, set up a display of souvenirs, or make a diorama.

FINAL POINTS ABOUT FIELD TRIPS

Field trips must be related to ongoing activities in the classroom (Hoover and Hollingsworth, 1982). If field trips are to be important and valuable to children, the trips should be planned in relation to ongoing activities in the classroom. Field trips can enrich children's study by providing learning experiences that are not possible through reading, discussion, or other classroom activities. Some field trips may be taken *near the beginning* of a unit for gathering information on specific topics or problems. Other field trips may be taken *during* the unit so that the children may get new ideas or different directions for their studies. A field trip may be taken *at the end* of a unit as a summarizing activity. Whenever the field trip is taken, it should be related to the classroom activities and *not* be an isolated "escape" from learning activities in the ongoing program.

Field trips must have a central point of interest. A central point of interest is a necessary ingredient for a successful field trip. And no matter where the trip may be, it is important that the trip meet the needs of the children involved and be of interest to them.

A preschool child will enjoy a *short, simple* trip to the fire station, police station, school nurse's office, dairy, local museum, library, or park. For early elementary children, the field trip could be to a museum, factory, planetarium, newspaper office, national forest, or other place where more complex activities may be observed. Whatever the trip's destination, there must be a *definite reason* for the visit.

Valuable socializing skills are learned on field trips. Many different goals can be achieved by field trips aside from gathering facts and observing activities first hand. For some children, the many activities engaged in as they work and socialize with one another on the field trip are as important as field trip facts and observations. Thus, a main point about field trips is the socialization that takes place among the children as they discuss, write about the activity, sit together on the bus, or ask questions of the guide.

The ideas on field trips in this unit are meant only as a beginning. Be flexible. Pick up cues from the children. Let them do some exploring, discovering on their own perhaps some of the very things built into the lesson plans for the trip. And if you find that the childrens'

POSITIVE	NEGATIVE
A field trip is realistic. The children have an opportunity to view and be a part of the real thing.	Field trips are time-consuming. If used extensively, they will definitely limit the content material that can be covered.
Inasmuch as the visit makes the experience real to the child, the field trip captures the interest and imagination of the learner.	Field trips may not be as successful as they might be because teachers develop inflexible habits of thinking about the learning/teaching processes. (Many teachers look at field trips as 30 children clustered together receiving a lecture.)
Field trips help children bridge the gap between school and real-life experiences.	
Field trips help develop language arts skills.	Many difficulties are encountered in managing and directing a group of children in a new and unfamiliar setting.
Field trips reduce the limiting qualities of school classrooms and buildings.	Sometimes field trips are seen by the children as a holiday from school.
Learning not easily visualized through reading, discussions, and classroom activities may be developed in a field trip.	Often children are pushed along in a large group and have no time to really see or ask, let alone explore.

FIGURE 10–9 Positive and negative aspects of field trips in the early childhood curriculum

interests take an entirely different bent, adjust the activity to go along with these immediate interests. As shown in Figure 10–9, the positive factors far outnumber the negative in providing young children with these outside-of-school learning experiences.

SUMMARY

Field trips are a way to introduce children to the wider world around them through first-hand experiences that cannot be brought into the classroom. Trips can be used to reinforce and extend concepts already learned. Field trips can also be used to focus on new ideas and concepts. Field trips need not be a one-shot visit, but may be several visits to the same location for different purposes.

Preparations for the time before, during, and after the field trip are necessary to making a field trip the kind of learning experience that justifies leaving the classroom to learn. Guidelines were suggested in this unit to consider in planning all field trips. Permission forms, Busy Bags for long bus trips, name tags, information on restroom facilities at the site to be visited, and other such information must all be obtained before the day of the trip.

As important as pretrip plans and a smooth trip itself is the posttrip period. At this time, it is important to send letters of thanks to the people involved in the trip, to discuss the trip with the children, to evaluate the trip, and to include the learnings in future lessons.

Field trips can be wonderful learning experiences for children. The positive aspects of field trips far outweigh the negative if the trips are handled properly.

LEARNING ACTIVITIES

A. Try to remember some school field trips you took as a young child. How do these trips compare to what you now know makes a worthwhile field trip? What do you remember most about those trips? Can you recall specific positive or negative feelings or occurrences from them? How can you use these personal remembrances in your own field trips as a teacher?

B. Select a subject area and grade level with which you are familiar. Using your own school community and the suggestions in your text, develop lesson plan goals for three possible class trips, one for *introducing* a lesson, one for *current learning,* and one for *practicing social skills.*

C. Read and comment on how the following relates to using neighborhood walks and children's interests as the bases for field trips:

> In the year 2101, Ellen's cousin, Joe, is visiting her from out of town. After exchanging family news, he says, "Listen, would you take me to see the electropods? I hear they're fantastic." Ellen stares at him in surprise. "Who would *ever* want to go *there?*" she asks. "Everyone knows what electropods look like." Joe goes into a dejected silence.

D. Take one phase of organizing a trip. Work out a checklist for yourself on this one phase. Share and compare your checklist with those of your fellow students.

E. Find out where parents of the children work. Choose one of these places for a field trip. Outline how you would go about organizing the trip. Be sure to include how it will fit into ongoing classroom units. Use the steps outlined in your text for the pretrip, actual trip, and posttrip planning stages.

F. Survey your local school community for nearby spots for field trips (preferably within walking distance). Share with your classmates several places you would visit, how they fit into ongoing classroom studies, and some pretrip preparations for each visit.

G. Using one of the following field trip locations, plan some pre- and posttrip activities for young children. Give the age group they are designed for.

Fire station	Craft fair
Police station	Dairy and other types of farms
Energy plant	Factory
Museum	Pet store
Farmer's market	Department store
Circus	Service station
Construction site	Restaurant

H. Information for this assignment may be obtained throughout the term rather than in a given week. Field trips are planned less frequently than other activities in the elementary program. When a number of students will be planning field trips for a single group of children, it is important that plans are closely coordinated with the teacher and spaced throughout the term. Adequate preparation and follow-up, as discussed in the unit, should be associated with each trip.

1. List the field trips that have been arranged for the group you work with during the term. Briefly describe those you have observed or participated in during your work with this group.
2. What limitations (if any) are placed on the group leaving the school? What time of day are they taken? How long should they last? How many adults are to be involved? Have the adults been advised of the particulars?
3. What purposes does the teacher have for planning field trips?
4. Give an example of the safety precautions taken for one field trip.
5. Make a plan for a field trip for your group of children. Make your plans around the steps discussed in the text. With your teacher's approval, carry out the plan for a few children or the whole group. Share your experiences.

I. Read the following account of a class trip by a child who went. Using the information in your text, find and list the points at which, as the teacher, you might have done things differently.

Yesterday we went to the planetarium with Ms. Haydock. It was fun, but not like I expected. Ms. Haydock said I couldn't take my camera because it might get lost or stolen, so I had to leave it in Mr. O's office. Then when we got on the bus she was real crabby. Some of the kids were sitting three in a seat, and she yelled at them. Jackie King stood up when we went around a corner, and he fell down and split his lip. The bus driver had a first-aid kit, but Ms. Haydock was yelling like crazy!

When we got to the planetarium we were too early for the show, so they wouldn't let us in. We were going to eat lunch afterward, but Ms. Haydock said we should do it now, so we went over to the park and started eating. I didn't want my sandwich so I started feeding it to the pigeons. Ms. Haydock came over and started shaking my arm and saying, "Don't be a litter-bug." When I tried to explain to her it was for the pigeons she just shook my arm some more.

Finally we went inside the planetarium and saw the show. It was sort of dumb. I didn't understand what they were talking about half the time. We never had that in Science class. The best part was when the lights went out, and I pinched Susie. She started crying and Ms. Haydock had to take her outside, so then we got to sit by ourselves and go "Ooooh" and whistle at the shooting stars. I saw one of the guards talking to Ms. Haydock later, and she looked like she wanted to cry.

When we got back on the bus, Mike Jones was missing. Ms. Haydock sent Buba to look for him, but then Mike came back and Buba was lost. Finally everyone was on the bus, and we drove back to school. We were so late I couldn't get my camera back, and my dad was so angry he shouted that he's going to school and tell that dumb teacher WHAT FOR.

I think the best part of the trip was when Jackie split his lip. I never saw so much blood in my life before.

ACTIVITIES FOR CHILDREN

Suggested Field Trips and Activities
Kindergarten/First Grade—Science
A. Unit: Our World in Autumn
B. Problem: What happens to leaves of trees and bushes and grass in the fall?
C. Concept: The leaves of many trees, grass, and bushes change in fall.
D. Trip: With a child-decorated paper bag, take a discovery walk in the playground or nearby neighborhood. Observe the change in leaves from trees and bushes and grass. Put samples in the bag for further activities in the classroom.

Any Elementary Grade Level—Music
A. Unit: Listening to Music
B. Problem: How many musical numbers can you identify?
C. Concept: Music with which the child can identify will aid her listening skills.

D. Trip: A young people's concert provides excellent opportunities for the children to apply good music listening skills. Music is played that appeals to them. Recordings of these pieces can be used in preparatory and follow-up activities in the classroom. A tape recorder might also be used at the concert.

Any Preschool or Elementary Grade Level –
Social Studies

A. Unit: The Grocery Store
B. Problem: To become aware of what a grocery store is and of how food is bought there. To see and name various kinds of fruit, etc.
C. Trip:
   1. Select any nearby grocery store. Select a time for your visit when the grocery store has relatively few customers.
   2. Be sure the children understand that the food is *for sale.* Take precautions against overhandling the produce or otherwise damaging store items.
   3. Keep the focus of the trip on a particular category of food and use it to extend the child's concept of the category by seeing and identifying items belonging to the category.

Any Preschool or Elementary Grade Level–
Social Studies

A. Unit: Follow-up Grocery Store Lesson
B. Problem: To become aware of other sections of the store; introducing other categories of food (vegetables, etc.)
C. Trip: Local grocery store. Visit other sections of the store, such as the bakery, canned goods, dairy products. Have the children help you shop for a few items.
D. Follow-up Activity: Cut out pictures from old magazines of goods and people seen at the grocery store. Help the children make a scrapbook. Encourage the child to talk about each picture and, if possible, write about her trips to the grocery store.

Preschool–Social Studies

A. Unit: Exploring a Department Store
B. Concept: To be aware of a department store and some things it sells. To ride on an escalator.
C. Trip:
   1. Select only a few things for the children to view and, when possible, to touch and manipulate.

Those merely viewed should be large objects that can be seen well from a distance and will hold the child's attention for a short time.
   2. If some children are frightened by the escalator or you feel it is safer, ride the elevator instead.
   3. Limit time spent in the store and leave before the children become fatigued or disinterested.
D. Follow-up Activities:
   1. Visit other kinds of stores: shoe stores, drugstores, and hardware stores.
   2. Help the children assemble a store for dramatic play.

Second and Third Grades–Language Arts

A. Unit: Newspapers for Reading
B. Problem: How is a newspaper printed?
C. Concept: Many steps and processes are necessary in printing a newspaper.
D. Trip: A trip to a plant where the newspapers are printed can help children see the processes from news reporting to printed paper.

Second and Third Grades–Science

A. Unit: Living Things in Our Environment (Plants and Animals)
B. Problem: Find evidences of living things in our neighborhood.
C. Concept: Living things around us everywhere in our environment.
D. Trip: Any outdoor park area provides ample opportunities for children to find many examples of living things.

Kindergarten through Third Grade–Art

A. Unit: Art Communicates a Story
B. Problem: What do these masterpieces of art say to you?
C. Concept: Art is a way of telling a story.
D. Trip: An art gallery can provide children with an opportunity to see how art communicates. Allow each child to see several (predetermined) masterpieces. Have the guide briefly tell the story of each picture.

Suggested Lesson Plans

Sample Lesson Plan–Billy the Kid Ballet

A. Objective: to prepare the class for the *Billy the Kid* ballet

B. Goals: Exposure and Recognition
  1. Billy the Kid, cowboys
  2. Ways of telling a story (the ballet)
  3. The music
  1. Billy the Kid
    a. Discuss the character (relate to other children they know who are twelve years old)
    b. Discuss cowboys, the Old West at the time of Billy the Kid
  2. Ways of telling a story
    a. Voice
    b. Dance: Discuss:

    • How the ballet will tell the story
    • How ballet involves training, practice, costumes
    • Use the book *A Young Dancer*
    • Use real toe shoes as visual aid

    c. Mime: Play "Guess My Mood" game where children take turns acting out an emotion, and the rest of the class tries to guess what it is.
  3. The music: *Billy the Kid* by Copeland
    a. Listen for mood
    b. Listen during rest time to the entire piece

Sample Lesson Plan–Social Studies

A. Problem: Why are rules, railroad signals, and signs needed at railroad crossings?
B. Concept: Rules, signals, and signs at railroad crossings are important for our safety.
C. Goals: After this lesson, the pupil should have greater understanding of safety around trains and railroad tracks, including rules, signals, and crossing signs, as evidenced by:
  1. Proper use of these devices during a field trip.
  2. Ability to discuss the purpose and meaning of signals and crossing signs during the field trip and follow-up activity in the classroom.
  3. Ability to write down the purpose under each sign.
  4. Participation in writing an experience story on safety rules.
D. Lesson Approach: Now that we have discussed the importance of railroad transportation to us and our country, what should we know about safety around trains? Have you ever been riding in a car and the car stopped so a train could cross the road? What would happen if the car did not stop? Why do we need rules for crossing the railroad tracks? What do these signs and signals mean? If no signs are by the railroad tracks, what safety rules should you follow?

Signs, signals, and rules of safety around railroad tracks are very important. We need to know these rules and what the signs and signals mean so we will not get hurt.
E. Planning: "What plans are necessary before we can take a field trip?" the teacher asks. The children would be guided to suggest necessary questions such as the following:

  1. Where could we see these railroad signals and signs?
  2. How could we get there?
  3. What could we do at the railroad tracks?
  4. When does the train pass by there?
  5. Who could tell us about the safety rules and railroad signals and signs?
  6. How can we tell our parents about a trip?

These questions and others could be discussed in the planning stages. The children could then be divided into groups and assigned specific tasks.
F. Field Trip: The trip will be made to a railroad station or depot. The guide will focus discussion at the site on safety rules, and the purposes for the railroad signs and signals. The children will be able to see how the signals and signs are used when trains approach. The children will demonstrate safety rules around trains and railroad tracks.
G. Evaluation Activities (Follow-up)

  1. Follow-up discussion concerning the purposes of rules and signals.
  2. Label each sign by giving its purpose.
  3. Write an experience story concerning the field trip emphasizing safety rules and the purposes of railroad signs and signals.
  4. Visit a train museum or display.

UNIT REVIEW

1. Outline brief lesson plans for the following field trips:
   a. Kindergarten to first grade—Science
   b. First to second grade—Math
   c. Second to third grade—Language Arts
   Include in your plans: Name of unit, problem, concept, and details of trip as covered in the suggested lesson plans at the end of this unit.
2. Discuss the benefits and disadvantages of field trips in the early childhood program.
3. List the three basic stages of all field trips. Give specific examples of activities from each stage based on your own experiences as well as from the text.
4. Explain why field trips must relate to ongoing classroom learning activities. Give examples of field trips that would relate to such ongoing activities from your own experience.

5. Why are pretrip plans and discussions with the class so important? What are some things to discuss with the children before any field trip? Would pretrip discussions be different for various trips? Explain.
6. How can you involve parents in field trips? Give examples of how you would include them in the pre- and posttrip activities, as well as on the field trip itself.
7. Using the information in your text and your own experience, respond to these statements:
   a. Field trips are more trouble than they're worth.
   b. All learning should take place outside the stuffy classroom.
   c. Field trips are a great way to have a nonschool holiday whenever you want one!

ADDITIONAL READINGS

Hoover, Kenneth H., and Hollingsworth, Paul M. *A Handbook for Elementary School Teachers.* Boston: Allyn and Bacon, 1982.

Ploghoft, M. and Shuster, A. *Social Science Education in the Elementary School,* 2nd Ed. Columbus, Ohio: Charles E. Merrill, 1976.

Taba, H., et al. *A Teacher's Handbook to Elementary Social Studies: An Inducative Approach.* Reading, Mass.: Addison-Wesley, 1971.

Walso, H.M. *Introducing the Young Child to the Social World.* New York: Macmillan, 1980.

Watrin, Rita, and Furfey, Paul Hanly. *Learning Activities for the Young Preschool Child.* New York: Van Nostrand, 1978.

Youniss, J. *Parents and Peers in Social Development.* Chicago: University of Chicago Press, 1980.

Appendix A
Fine and Gross Motor Skills*

BY SIX YEARS

Gross Motor
- Skips, both feet (average age five years)
- Hops 5 yards forward, either foot (by age six*)
- Two-handed catch of tennis ball, after single bounce; eight out of ten tries (average age five years)
- Balances standing on one foot, 10 seconds (average age four and one-half years)

Fine Motor
- Draws a man, six parts (average age four and three-quarter years)
- Strings eight beads in 25 seconds (by age six*)

BY SEVEN YEARS

Gross Motor
- Balances on one foot 20 seconds, with arms upraised
- Walks forward 10 steps heel to toe, keeping balance
- Balances on tiptoes, bending forward from hips
- Marches, skips to rhythm

Fine Motor
- Copies diamond from picture model
- Knows right and left on self
- Can knit eyebrows (frown)
- Sorts 36 playing cards into four piles in 30 seconds

BY EIGHT YEARS

Gross Motor
- Jumps sideways, feet together, three successive jumps of about 12–14 inches
- Stork balance: stands on one foot with sole of other foot against supporting knee, 20 seconds; one of two trials
- Crouches on tiptoes, 10 seconds one of three trials
- Catches, on the fly, a tennis ball bouncing off a wall from a distance of 8 feet; underhand throw, two-handed catch, four out of ten trials

Fine Motor
- Touches thumb to tip of all fingers of one hand successively in 5 seconds; one of two tries
- Can wrinkle the forehead; lift eyebrows

BY NINE YEARS

Gross Motor
- Jumps and claps twice before landing
- Balances standing on one foot, eyes closed
- Catches an underhand-thrown tennis ball, one-handed, from distance of 8 feet; six of ten trials
- Jumps over rope 40 cm. high

Fine Motor
- Flexes and extends feet

BY TEN YEARS

Gross Motor
- Balances on tiptoes, eyes closed, 15 seconds
- Jumps and claps three times before landing
- Jumps, feet together, over rope at knee height, lands on one foot and balances 5 seconds; one out of two tries, each foot

Fine Motor
- Closes the eyes alternately

*Ninety percent of children at specified age level will have acquired the skill.

Adapted from Gesell, Arnold; Ilg, Frances L.; Ames, Louise Bates; and Rodell, Janet Leonard. *Infant and Child in the Culture of Today: The Guidance of Development in Home and Nursery School.* New York: Harper and Row, 1974.

Index